The Care of Pictures

By GEORGE L. STOUT

DOVER PUBLICATIONS, INC.
NEW YORK

Published in Canada by General Publishing Company, Ltd., 30 Lesmill Road, Don Mills, Toronto,
Ontario.
Published in the United Kingdom by Constable
and Company, Ltd., 10 Orange Street, London WC 2.

This Dover edition, first published in 1975, is an
unabridged republication of the work originally
published by the Columbia University Press in
1948, to which have been added a New Preface to the
Dover Edition and Revised Bibliography prepared
by the author.

International Standard Book Number: 0-486-23165-8
Library of Congress Catalog Card Number: 74-25487

Manufactured in the United States of America
Dover Publications, Inc.
180 Varick Street
New York, N.Y. 10014

Preface to the Dover Edition

URING almost twenty-five years since the following pages were composed, many changes and many advances have occurred in the professional practice of conservation of works of art. Those have only a slight bearing on the content of these following pages. The writing was addressed not to the person who practices conservation as a profession but rather to the person who, as owner or as custodian, is responsible for the safe keeping of pictures. The few particulars that should be modified or corrected can be marked without need of resetting the type where they are found.

The Preface, p. vi, says that no recognized system of training had been provided for professional conservators. Since 1948 many centers for such training have been provided. Moreover, a stable professional organization has reached around the world. Established under British charter, it carries the name, International Institute for the Conservation of Artistic and Historic Works. Fellows of the Institute (IIC) are the qualified body of professional conservators.

On pages 11 and 12 the binding mediums mentioned have been increased in number by synthetic compounds. Acrylics are now sold along with oil and water colors. There will be more, but these have not yet produced their category of problems in the care of pictures.

A method of improving the condition of a varnish coating by exposure to solvent vapor, pages 19–21, is called "regeneration," being translated literally from the German name given to it in 1864. Elizabeth Jones (*On Picture Varnishes and their Solvents*, Cleveland and London, 1971), chooses to call it "re-forming."

On pages 24 and 45 the time interval of twenty years could now be doubled.

In Appendix B, on special means of examination, many additions would be needed to bring the list up to date: neutron activation autoradiography, chromatography, laser radiation and X-ray diffraction on extracted samples are among them. There has been a large change in methods of examination by infra-red illumination and some change in the interpretation of fluorescence under ultra-violet light. Many of these have been recognized in the revised bibliography. They have broadened the knowledge of professional conservators but they have not greatly changed the ordinary procedures in the care of pictures.

GEORGE L. STOUT

Menlo Park, California
July 12, 1971

Preface to the First Edition

THE MEN who made pictures during past centuries would have found it hard to believe the truth if anybody could have told them what lay ahead for their works. Many of those have been lost, but a good many have been saved from fire, flood, war, and from weather and worms and mold. They have been moved on cars pulled by steam, they have been flown in aircraft, hidden a thousand feet below ground, sold for sums that in other days would have bought a kingdom, lighted by energy that flows through wires, recorded by hundreds of photographs, and reproduced on the pages of books. And their designers in other times would have been confounded by the means now taken to preserve those works.

The aim of this piece of writing is not to review the means of preservation or conservation now at hand for pictures; this is not to be a technical work. It is to be a summary of information, put together and explained as briefly as seemed possible, for any persons who may have something to do with the care of any kind of pictures—the artists who make them, the students who are learning that craft, the curators or keepers responsible for such objects, and the collectors or householders who have them around. It is merely an introduction to problems in the care of pictures, and the hope is that it may prove to be a useful introduction.

It will be of little or no use to the professional conservator, for nothing in it is new to him. His handbook, if it ever gets written, will be quite different from this. The expert, the professional, and his vocation are not widely understood, and, as he is mentioned fairly often in the following pages, it would be well to say something about him. He is not cast in a mold; temperaments and capabilities cover a wide range. A generation ago he was called "restorer," and some still prefer this title. It is too pretentious for others. It implies operation that is just short of magic—treatment of a picture to bring it back to its original state. Nobody literally restores a picture. The most that any operator can do is to stave off the working of those agencies that would injure it and to recover what is left of its character.

The name is a secondary matter. The qualifications of the conservator are primary and are important, and there is little to guide an owner or curator when he looks for expert professional help. It is not a licensed profession. There is no law to prevent any man from calling himself by such a name or from undertaking such work. Perhaps that is just as well since it is a numerically small vocation and no recognized system of training has been provided for it. But, without limits set, there are bound to be wide differences in competence, and how is a responsible person to judge between better and worse? Keep in mind certain accepted propositions: that action in matters of conservation needs to be founded on knowledge of works of art and on knowledge of the materials that compose them—real knowledge, not rule of thumb or theory or shop habit or old wives' talk; that what is done to a picture during treatment or repair may decide its lasting condition and its ultimate appearance; and that in the work of conservation a selection must be made among all the means available —in all the known art and technology of the time—for improving the condition of a picture. The manifold prospects and risks and chances must be reckoned. With these propositions in mind, consider whether or not a man who calls himself a conservator or a restorer seems to have the knowledge that his occupation needs. Is he a person of good education, of sound judgment, and of reasonable inclinations? Does he explain his work in a way that is frank and rational, or does he hide behind affectations of peculiar taste and sensibility? Does he maintain full records? Does he insist on complete exploration of the condition and is he clear about the facilities for examination—physical, optical, chemical, and photographic?

Description of these facilities has been deliberately kept out of the following chapters and a list of the means of technical examination added in an appendix. Unless they were segregated that way, they seemed likely to cause confusion. These instruments can be found only in laboratories, and they can be used only by experts. During recent years their importance has probably been exaggerated, especially in studies of the authenticity of objects. Ultraviolet and infrared light, X rays, and the others were supposed to be new and fierce tools, and they were expected to show the truth. They have brought into view certain kinds of facts, and among these are facts that have value in the study of the condition of pictures. A competent conservator will know whether or not he needs the facts that might be provided by these facilities and how to appraise those facts after they are before him.

Competence is never easy to find, and competent workmanship in conservation is tedious and expensive. Probably there are many pictures that are not worth it, but that is a hard judgment to make. An owner can say, "It belongs to me and I'll take a chance." This is an area where values shift and judgments fail because there are no definite weights and measures. For some things the count is pretty well settled. They are labeled as great, and the mark of universal esteem is on them. An owner has a legal title to them, but with it goes a social responsibility. If he wants to think himself a responsible member of society, he can not willfully take chances with things like that.

It may stand as gross negligence to have written even a very short book that has to do with pictures and in it to have said nothing about their value to the worried people of the earth. This, as the standard comment runs, is not the place. The means of saving these things need to be studied in cold blood and understood as matters of structure and mechanics. Action must be planned and carried out on that kind of appraisal. But have it planned and carried out, if the work is to get its fairest chance, by those who know the value and the quality of the things they work with, who highly respect that value and are devoted to seeing it preserved. Without such devotion there may not be the will to exhaust all means that can be found or the patience to keep on to the last conceivable step in finishing the job.

The plan of these few chapters is made according to the main structural divisions in pictures. This was done with the aim of keeping the construction always in view. Unless that is clear, the problems of conservation can not be understood. Because of this plan some repetition will be noticed. Certain identical agents of damage and deterioration work at different levels in the construction, and it seemed better to deal with them as they came, even though they turned up two or three times. Let it be kept quite definite that this is not a technical handbook on conservation. Its purpose is to survey the field, to review some of the problems, and to suggest a few principles and means of general care. The records given in Appendix A are put there to represent briefly a small number of laboratory procedures. They are not directions or operating methods. The Bibliography is not critical; it shows some of the sources of information, better and worse, which in detail relate to the care of pictures.

For the writer, the main source, however, has been in years of study and practice with able and friendly associates in the Department of Conservation at the Fogg Museum of Art, Harvard University. They would not want to be named. They know what they have contributed, and they know that it will never be forgotten.

GEORGE L. STOUT

Worcester, Massachusetts
February 10, 1948

Contents

List of Figures

List of Plates

The Care of Pictures

1 · Construction of Pictures

THINGS break or change because the materials in them get worn or injured or because they fade, rot, or corrode. Damage and decay can not be prevented altogether, but if the materials and the construction of a thing can be understood and if the sources of possible deterioration are kept in mind, much can be done to hold things in a good state. The materials in pictures may be complex in their nature, and the way they are put together in a construction may be even more complex, but the main kinds of picture materials and building can be simply described and broadly understood.

If you take a piece of paper and make a mark on it with a piece of charcoal, you have, in about the simplest terms, the structural parts of a picture. In this the paper serves as a support, the thing on which the picture is carried, and the charcoal will do to represent the other structural part, the design. A great many pictures have been made since the earliest recorded times and are still being made with only these two main parts. The charcoal alone is a pigment, one form of carbon black. Substitute for it a mixture of pigments and add enough sticking material to hold these mixed powders in place after they are dry, and you have paint. If the sticking or binding material is gum arabic, you have so-called "water color" (Figure 2). Add to the charcoal other colors in powder or made up in sticks, put them on dry, and you have approximately the kind of construction called "pastel." Add oil to the powdered charcoal and print with this mixture from a block or plate, and you have the whole range of the graphic arts, wood block, etching, lithograph, and the others.

Recall to mind the kinds of pictures you know and have seen, and you will remember that a fairly large number of materials has been used as supports to carry them. In the Low Countries during the sixteenth century, copper flattened into sheets was often painted on. At about the same time in northern Italy, stone was frequently used. Ivory became a regular support for miniature painting. There has been extensive painting on leather, glass, various metals, various preparations of skins, terra cotta, plaster, dry clay, and numerous synthetic materials. The most common supports, however, are wood, fabric, and paper. All of these are organic materials and all are somewhat alike, for they share the basic substance, cellulose. In paper and fabric the fibers have been removed from their original position of growth and have been twisted, woven, or felted into new relations (Figure 1).

In wood the original arrangement of the cells remains. Most of these long, tubular cells are in a relatively parallel position; they may be large or small, depending on the time when they were formed, large, thin-walled cells having grown in the spring. The alternation of rings of spring wood and the more dense summer wood produces the grain in a cut piece of wood, and grain influences splitting, checking, warping, and a somewhat irregular response of wood to conditions of the atmosphere. Wood is a strong stuff, particularly resistant to any pressure at right angles to the direction of its grain. It can be worked conveniently with simple hand tools. It can be made flat and suitable for use as a painting support in normal sizes. Its weight is moderate. The great defects of wood, as a picture support, are its tendency to warp or split along the lines of the grain and its tendency to be infested by insects.

Fabric, as ordinarily used to support pictures, has a simple weave and a strong thread. In the West, linen is the most common; in the Far East, silk. By itself a fabric has fairly strong resistance to agencies of deterioration. The materials that are put on fabric, either to prepare it for use in a more convenient way or to repair it at some later time, have caused weakening in this kind of picture support. Even an untreated fabric may get moldy and will in time become brittle from

Relation of fibers in wood

Position of summer-wood vessel

Fibers are parallel; wood grain runs the long way of them

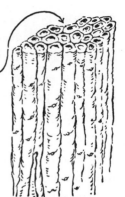

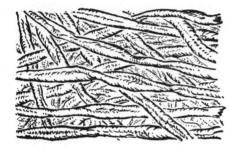

Separated fibers, tangled, massed, or felted, as seen at the surface of paper

Twisted fibers that form the threads of a woven fabric

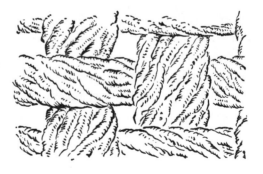

FIGURE I · FIBER ARRANGEMENT IN
COMMON PICTURE SUPPORTS

oxidation. But both of these are accelerated by the addition of sizing materials, particularly animal glue. Glue shrinks and swells in changes of humidity, it gets brittle, and it grows mold quickly when damp.

Similar applications have damaged a great deal of the paper used to support pictures. But in the case of paper it is necessary to distinguish between two different kinds of fiber used in the manufacture. The rag paper, which has always been considered superior in European and American work, is made from cotton or linen rags which have been softened and macerated until the separate fibers are teased out and later floated and felted into a sheet form. What is sometimes called "pulp" paper comes from wood fiber either ground or separated by chemical treatment. Ground-up wood, mechanical pulp, used in newsprint, in cheap paper, or in cardboard, has caused a great deal of trouble as a picture support or as a mount for works on thin paper since it came into use in the late eighteenth century. It contains the entire wood substance. It discolors and carries a discoloration into adjacent material. Mold grows in it readily. Paper figures in the appearance of many kinds of pictures that are made on this material as a support. It is part of the design in drawings and prints and usually in water colors. Paper or silk takes a like place in the ink paintings of China and Japan and in the paintings of India and the Near East. All these are simple constructions, and in them the support is the base tone on which they are developed. If that changes, the picture is inevitably damaged. In every case the strength or weakness of the support and its tendency to remain flat have an influence on the picture and on its survival.

Instead of making a mark with charcoal directly on a piece of paper, suppose that you had decided that the paper as it stood was not suitable, that it was too rough or too porous or too soft and that the charcoal required a stronger surface to take it smoothly. To get this you might have mixed some white, powdered chalk with a very weak glue and have spread and smoothed it over the paper. In so doing you would have laid on the support what is technically called a "ground." Papers with grounds are used for pastel and for silver point, the direct, delicate drawing with metallic silver. The use of grounds brings in a somewhat more complex type of picture construction, for the ground is by definition and general understanding never a direct part of the design. It is a smooth, flat coating put over the support. For the most part the ground is a device of European painters. It may have come into wide use during the Middle Ages when much of the surface of a painted panel carried gold leaf and when a very smooth preparation was needed to imbed this leaf and to permit burnishing and tooling it (Figure 2).

The color or tone of grounds is usually white or light. This allows for easy development of the drawing. The material which gives this tone is a white powder, and many such materials have been used for the purpose: gypsum, chalk, China clay, and white pigments. To make the powder hold in a firm layer on the support, some kind of binder or adhesive is needed, and the usual one is a skin glue or any animal glue. The reason for the choice of a water-soluble adhesive is largely that it works better—dries quicker and smooths more easily—and also that it keeps the white tone of such inert materials as gypsum or chalk. These look drab and brown when mixed with oils. Oil grounds can be made, however, with white pigments such as white lead or zinc or titanium white, often mixed with chalk or another inert filler, and are now fairly common on prepared artists' canvas. Probably the greatest cause of deterioration in the older, aqueous grounds is the presence of glue which reacts quickly to changes in relative humidity and is a good food for mold and microorganisms. There is less glue in canvas supports that have oil grounds, but often glue is used on these as a sizing before the ground is laid.

In a structural sense there is no difference between a ground and a paint. The different terms merely indicate different functions or uses in the construction of a picture. Ground is a smooth, even coat

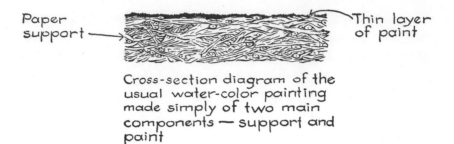

Paper support → ← Thin layer of paint

Cross-section diagram of the usual water-color painting made simply of two main components — support and paint

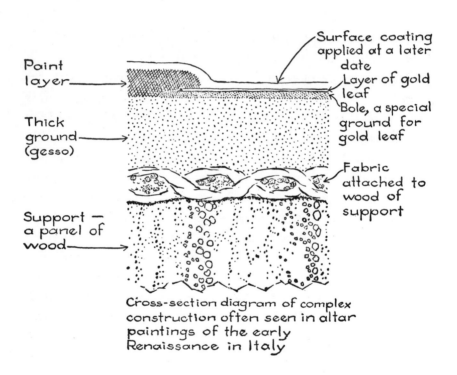

Surface coating applied at a later date

Paint layer →

Layer of gold leaf

Bole, a special ground for gold leaf

Thick ground (gesso) →

Fabric attached to wood of support

Support — a panel of wood →

Cross-section diagram of complex construction often seen in altar paintings of the early Renaissance in Italy

FIGURE 2 · SIMPLE AND COMPLEX
CONSTRUCTION OF PICTURES

the purpose of which is largely mechanical. The paint, whether applied by a stick, a brush, a pen, or a printing press, contains the drawing and development of the pictorial idea. Whether the material is ground or paint, it is usually composed of two very different substances—the pigment and the binding material. The difference between these two components needs to be kept clear because there is a tendency to use the word "pigment" in place of the word "paint." Paint, to repeat, is a mixture of pigment and medium. Pigments have to be thought of as powders. Seen under a microscope they are lumps or grains. To get a clear idea of a paint film or paint layer, imagine chunks of coal piled together in a shallow box with some kind of sticky material like tar to hold them together. This is essentially the appearance of a paint film when studied under a microscope. If the coal is relatively large in quantity and there is only enough tar to cement it at adjacent edges, the mixture is lean. If there is an oversupply of tar, so much that it flows over the tops of the lumps and the lumps themselves float in it, the relation would resemble that of a rich paint (Figure 3). Lean paint is mat and granular. It is found in most wall painting and in pastels. Rich paint is glossy and smooth. It is found in the translucent glazes of some painting done with oil as a medium.

Pigment materials are many and varied, and little would be gained by catalogue or a long description of them. Some are taken directly from the earth. Certain of these are colored by iron, yellow, brown, or red; they are ochers and umbers. Some are synthetic preparations like white lead or cobalt blue, and among these pigments are those that go back in time to ancient Egypt. Some are dyes precipitated on a base, like the old madder or the modern alizarin crimson. All come to the paint maker or to the painter as powders, and these have to be combined with some kind of medium, a material that will bind them in a layer and will hold them where they belong in the design.

Throughout the Far East the common adhesive or binding me-

White chalk (pigment) lodges on
a support of slate without
any binding medium

Pigment particles

Slate

Lean paint has only enough
binding medium to hold
pigment in place

Pigment particles

Medium

Ground

A large amount of medium
in proportion to pigment
makes a rich paint

Pigment

Medium

Ground

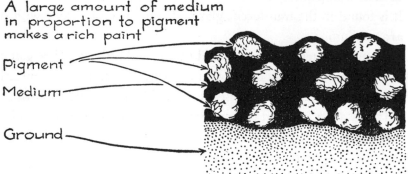

FIGURE 3 · PIGMENT AND MEDIUM
MAGNIFIED CROSS SECTIONS

dium for paint is the same as that for the ink of India and China, an animal glue. The source of glue or gelatin is collagen, the organic material of bones, tendons, cartilage, and skin. These substances, heated in water, give a gelatin solution. It is used in relatively small quantity as related to the carbon black of the ink, and the mixture itself is therefore lean. Lacquer, however, the poisonous sap of the *Rhus vernicifera* DC, is also a binding medium well known in Asia, and lacquer, as usually worked, is a paint. The number of materials used for mediums in Europe has been greater probably than in the Far East. Egg yolk and egg white, gum arabic, exuded by the acacia tree, and finally the drying oils have been added to the more ancient glues and waxes. Oil as a binding medium may have come into use in the early Middle Ages. By the fifteenth century it was well known. It probably had a number of sources—walnuts, poppy seeds, and flax seeds or linseeds. To be satisfactory as a medium an oil must be able to dry, to change from a fluid layer to a hard film. This is brought about not by evaporation and return to a hard state, as in glue or gum, but by a chemical change in the presence of air—an oxidation and polymerization. Oils so constructed that they can make this change are drying oils. It is a common failing of all such materials, since all of them are organic in nature, to deteriorate and become weak and brittle. Those which are mixed with water at the time of application are subject to the action of water at later times and are also subject to damage by mold. Oil is only moderately susceptible to mold growth and very slightly to water, but it follows a constant course of oxidation which renders it more brittle, more translucent, and more yellow as time goes on. Of all the known binding materials East and West, lacquer and wax seem to have the nearest approach to permanence.

The kind of picture familiar as an oil painting in the Western world is regularly coated with a film-forming substance or mixture referred to as a varnish. The word "varnish" is ordinarily related, however, to those film materials that are made of resin or of mixed oil and resin.

There is less confusion if all substances which may be used for the outer, transparent coating of a picture are designated by the term "surface coating." Under this term other materials—synthetic resins, pure oils, and waxes—can be included. The numbers and origins of materials which have been used traditionally in the compounding of surface coatings are beyond the reach and far beyond the necessity of description. Among the oils have been chiefly those of linseed, walnut, poppy seed, soya bean, and China wood; among waxes have been beeswax, paraffin, ceresin, and carnauba; among resins have been the hard fossils, amber and copal, and the soft resins—mastic, dammar, and sandarac. These are the names of only a few, and there is a wide range of mixtures and of combination in different layers. A kind of sentimental association goes with some of these materials—oil from Calcutta, amber from the shore of the Baltic, and copal from Zanzibar—but they have their practical drawbacks. The difficulty with a drying oil, as this must be noticed in the care of pictures, has already been mentioned—its tendency to get brittle and dark with age. The same tendency to deteriorate is found in the resins and in them is much greater.

Wall painting has not been considered thus far, and this is a kind of picture construction that seldom has to be handled. Broadly, there are two kinds. In one, the wall itself can be considered as a support, the plaster as a ground, and the paint as a mixture of pigment with weak glue applied over the plaster ground. This is the common construction of wall painting in the Far East. In the West a different type of construction developed, that is called "fresco." In its pure state this has no binding medium as such. The pigment is mixed with water to permit its application and in that mixture is put on the wet plaster which has to be a lime hydrate. As this dries and takes up carbon dioxide from the air, it recrystallizes and the pigment particles, spread on its surface as design, are locked among the crystals that form. This kind of picture is as strong as the plaster and the wall behind it, and subject to the same causes of damage—cracking, wear, and the action of impurities in the air.

Many terms have been tried as labels for picture construction, but few of them have any meaning that will help to define materials or to explain how they are put together or to indicate how they are to be preserved. The word "gouache," for example, has been applied to a particular type of construction in which tinted paper is the support, on which—as a rule—there is no ground, and in which the paint is mixed with an aqueous medium like gum arabic. This is not very different from so-called "water color," and practically it is no different as to requirements for its care. The support is tinted, and some white probably is mixed with the colors. Still it is an aqueous paint on a paper support. The word "tempera" could be applied to it with about the same accuracy. Care of a thing like this, or of anything so made, needs a workable comprehension of how paper is built and of how the paint lies on it and of what may happen to cause a defect in any of the materials of construction.

2 · Surface Blemishes

As soon as a picture is finished, it starts to deteriorate. Those first few days or months are the only time in its whole history when its condition is perfect. The changes in it will be produced by inevitable circumstances and by chance acting on the materials from which it is made. The rate of its change will depend a good deal on the relation of the picture's surface to conditions in the air, on its ability to withstand dust, wear, injurious gases, light, and dampness. In Asia it has been the practice to put things away, somewhat removed from these conditions. Movable pictures are laid in covers or rolled and kept in boxes. In the West certain kinds of pictures, like prints and drawings, are kept boxed or, like water colors and pastels, are regularly shielded in frames behind glass. Other kinds are coated with varnish. The use of varnish or of some surface coating has increased as cities have become more smoky and as the need for it has become more evident. There are good signs that painted altarpieces, even before the time when oil got to be the prevailing medium, did not always carry a surface coating.

The traditional coating for the surface of a picture is varnish, made by dissolving or fusing a natural resin in a fluid that will let it be brushed. A resin is produced directly by a plant. Usually it comes from a living tree, but buried, fossil resins are from trees long dead. Formed in special glands of the tree, the resinous fluid is usually collected from slashes or wounds in the bark. It hardens in the air. Chemically, the resins are complex. They contain various acids, resinols, resino-tannols, resenes, and essential oils, and chemically they are different among themselves. They look much alike, and their appearance is familiar to everyone who has seen chunks of rosin. The common rosin, called "colophony" in the trade, is derived from the balsam of pine trees. This is very rarely used in picture varnishes, but its origin is the same as those resins—mastic, dammar, sandarac, and the fossils—which go to make up the usual varnishes. Although the trees that furnish them are of many species and far apart geographically, the resins have a number of common characteristics. They have a glassy structure. They can be melted by heat, are not dissolved in water, and are fairly resistant to chemical reagents and to the micro-organisms or molds that cause decay.

The kinds of resins that may have been used in the past are fairly large in number. For convenience they are put into two broad classes: hard and soft. Copal and amber are hard resins. They need to be fused, melted in oil at a high temperature, to get them into a fluid and ready for application. That is the traditional means of preparation, and copal at least has been much used in the past. It is a fossil resin, as a rule, though some varieties are taken directly from the wood. The hardest copal comes from Zanzibar and the fossil is dug from the earth in other parts of Africa and in South America, New Zealand, and the East Indies. Amber, the same material used for jewelry, comes mainly from the area of the Baltic Sea. Both of these fossil resins make varnishes that are strong when put on, very hard to dissolve after drying, and, originally dark in color, grow darker with age. The soft resins can be dissolved in organic solvents, and because of that the solution is often called "spirit varnish." Some go into turpentine and other hydrocarbons; some work better in alcohols. Most of them are from the Mediterranean region or from the Far East. One of the two most common is mastic, found in Portugal, Morocco, and the Canary Islands in small quantities but mainly from one island, Chios, in the Greek Archipelago. The other common soft resin is dammar, taken from a tree grown in the Malay States and in the East Indies.

Whether it is hard or soft, oil-fused or spirit-dissolved, the resin produces a film that is only more or less clear. At best, it has some color and some slight cloudiness. In a thin layer this does not show and, when first put on, a varnish can be considered as a transparent film like glass. Before many years, however, clarity diminishes. The glass seems to be colored yellowish brown. It may get faint bluish streaks, and it begins to look rough, shot through with cracks, and ends by being a kind of veil or screen rather than a clear film. The deterioration of varnishes made out of natural resins is quick or slow, covers a few years or many years, partly in consequence of the kind of resin used and partly as a result of housing—general cleanliness, light, and relative dryness. The phenomena of deterioration have been studied with much care, and the basic causes are considered to be oxidation, or autoxidation, molecular rearrangement and association, and the loss of volatile essential oils.

Blemishes and discoloration in surface coatings can be noticed by one or more of three different attributes or earmarks. The first, and the easiest to explain, is the ordinary accumulation of dust or grime from the air. Whatever settles on the wall around a picture naturally tends to settle on the picture also. If the varnish is slick, dust will be apt to drop off or fail to lodge there in the first place. But some will stick, and it may hold tightly enough once it has got fixed in place. A speck of dust may become a small focus for condensation of atmospheric moisture, and certainly dampness improves the chances for a surface to hold any grime that may come its way.

The second earmark of deterioration is darkening. Practically nothing can be done to prevent this as long as the material is in contact with the air. Many of the soft resins are mixed with small amounts of oil to reduce their brittleness, the hard or fossil resins have been fused with oil in their preparation, and the complex process of darkening in oil adds itself to that of the resins in most picture coatings. Darkening as such can usually be gauged by looking at the relative value of a white area in a picture, a lace or linen cuff or frill, a highlight, or a cloud. Hold a white handkerchief beside one of these spots and notice how near it comes to reflecting the same amount of light. Along with the natural darkening of the materials of surface coatings goes the stain that was often put into them when they were made up and applied. In the technological history of European painting there is not much to show that varnishing of pictures, as an application to the whole surface, was a fixed practice until late, perhaps the seventeenth century. There are few pictures to be seen today which still carry varnish as old as that. In most, the surface coatings have been taken off and replaced. Often blemishes were found in the paint underneath or there were uneven streaks of grime which were not removed. It seems to have been a common practice to smooth out breaks and irregularities by tinting the varnish with a thin, weak stain. Occasionally this is found in an independent layer, a pale brown scumble put over a whole surface. More often it is an actual coloring put into the first layer of the surface coating. Some of the artists and artisans who have worked on pictures frankly resorted to this treatment as a means of saving time and pleasing the owner. The coloring of the varnish was known in the workshops by various names such as "Old Master Glow" or "Toner."

A third type of blemish is somewhat broadly spoken of as bloom. The word has never been given any very precise meaning. It is used to describe an effect—a dull, whitish, foggy appearance. The word "clouding" would define it better. With this appearance goes a loss of transparency. Different kinds and degrees of such a loss are evident, and there are different explanations for their cause. All of them, however, come in some way from a break-down of the smooth, uniform consistency in the coating. This may be from chemical or merely from mechanical causes. The result is about the same. Instead of having a single, clean plane of reflecting surface like that on a pool of still water, you have one which is broken like the surface of sand. Light can not travel through it in straight lines (Figure 4). In some

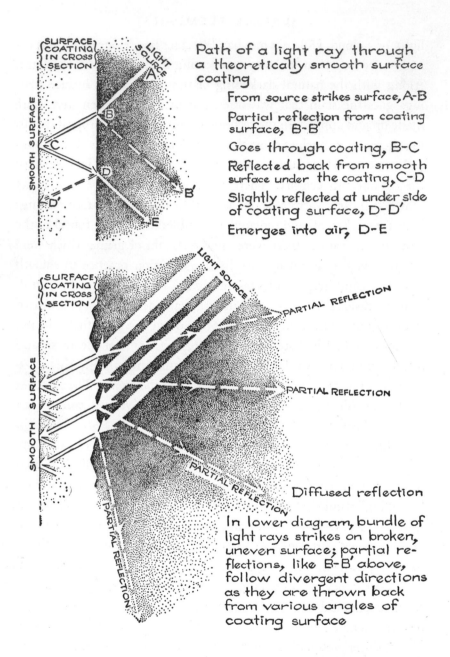

Path of a light ray through a theoretically smooth surface coating

From source strikes surface, A-B

Partial reflection from coating surface, B-B'

Goes through coating, B-C

Reflected back from smooth surface under the coating, C-D

Slightly reflected at under side of coating surface, D-D'

Emerges into air, D-E

Diffused reflection

In lower diagram, bundle of light rays strikes on broken, uneven surface; partial reflections, like B-B' above, follow divergent directions as they are thrown back from various angles of coating surface

FIGURE 4 · REFLECTION ON SURFACES

cases it can not get through at all. The difference between this and a fresh coating is the difference between ice and snow. Dampness condensed in such a film increases the disturbance and at times has produced a complete blanching until a coating looks as if it were white paint. Practically, different degrees of clouding, of dullness and opacity, in a surface coating go with long-term drying and reorganization of the film structure. The film breaks up and is hard to see through because it has become brittle and is cut by minute cracks (Figure 5 and Plate I). The stiff, vitreous character of an old resin coating makes it easily subject to small damages. It can be scarred by a finger nail. Even the tip of a finger rubbed across it may cause a whitish streak. Whether it is fresh or old, a varnish is easily scratched. These surface defects are apt to be only skin deep. They may be disturbing to the eye, they may partly obscure a picture, but, unless they have actually penetrated into the paint layer, they will have done no permanent damage and they can be removed.

Treatment or repair of surface coatings runs all the way from the simplest dusting to complete removal. It could be said that many of the steps in such treatment, those which do not come down to work on the paint itself, could safely be taken by any person not trained in conservation. The trouble is that before it is safe to touch a surface of varnish over the paint, the condition of the paint and its tightness to the ground and the support under it must be appraised and understood. Otherwise, permanent damage might be done. Except for dusting, any treatment of varnish had better be made a job for an expert. Methods of treating a surface coating are beyond number in all of their possible combinations, but, among all these, two basic measures are known: a regeneration process and removal.

The word "regeneration" is probably a poor one. It was translated literally from the German *Regenerationsverfahren* or *Regenerierungsverfahren*. The procedure might be better indicated as softening or plasticizing. It was expounded chiefly by Max von Pettenkofer,

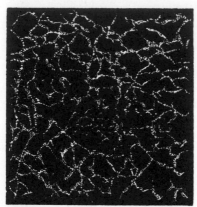

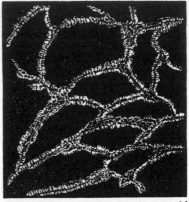

Under a magnifying glass the clouded area is seen to have a fine network of cracks (crazing)

Further magnified, small shell-like fractures become evident along the cracks in the coating

At high magnification the shell-like fractures show a further crazing; these complex breaks reflect and refract light in a way to cause the appearance of clouding

FIGURE 5 · CLOUDING OF A RESIN COATING

and the process is often given his name. In this type of treatment the surface film is left alone for the most part, and the broken granules are at least partly dissolved and re-established as a unified mass. This is done by exposing the picture to alcohol vapor in a tight box. No solvent which can be applied in vapor form does much to change a hard or fossil resin after that has become thoroughly aged. Dried oils do not respond to even the strongest of organic solvents, and the hard resins with them are about equally impervious. If they could be dissolved, there would be no reason for fusing them in oil, a tedious process, at the time when they are made. Soft resins in a solvent vapor will react by going into solution more or less rapidly and more or less completely (Figure 6, Appendix A, 6, and Plate XVI). If the kind and condition of the surface coating are favorable to vapor solution, the film is recovered as a fairly uniform, thin mass with an improved reflecting surface. The color of the coating will not be much changed, and if artificial coloring, such as stain or pigment, has been added, vapor treatment is apt to cause a kind of splotchiness of the surface. At best, the softening process is a temporary gain. As soon as the solvent has been lost by evaporation, deterioration sets in again rapidly.

The other fundamental type of treatment for surface coatings, and a great deal the more common one in practice, is removal. Ordinarily this is done by dissolving the resin in an appropriate solvent (Appendix A, 1, 2, and 4, and Plates II and III). Other methods have been talked about a good deal, but it is doubtful if they have been much used by experienced persons. This is the part of the conservation of paintings which seems to have been the favorite area for old home remedies and quaint nostrums. Some will say, and with great sincerity, that there is only one proper way to remove old varnish and that is to break it up with a dull tool and brush it off. Others will claim that the surface must first be washed with soap and water and will let it be known that the water has to stand in a certain kind of

Effect of solvent vapor on a broken coating of mastic resin as seen in a magnified field

Before exposure to concentrated fumes of morpholene

Sharp edges of broken resin

Fine striation in fracture

Scattering of small broken pieces

After one minute of exposure

Edges blurred

Striation fused

Small broken pieces partly dissolved

After five minutes of exposure

Edges lost except of main fracture

Striation all dissolved

Small pieces taken up in condensed fluid of solution

FIGURE 6 · SOLUTION OF VARNISH

pot and the soap must be cooked during the dark of the moon. The trained conservator has means of laboratory examination to settle his questions concerning the solubility of a surface coating and the condition and strength of the original paint. Suitable solvents or solvent mixtures can ordinarily be found on the basis of such an investigation, and the methods of applying the solvents, taking up the dissolved resins, and proceeding over the whole work can be developed according to the needs of each case. That is generally the way removal is done. It is slow work and often complicated by layers of overpaint (Plate XIII).

In any well-organized procedure of this kind, the material that is taken off is known to be foreign to the picture before it is removed. A great deal of misunderstanding has developed in a few cases because persons who had known a picture during all their lives had grown accustomed to it in a discolored state. When the discoloration was removed, the character of the picture was completely changed for them. They were shocked by the change and naturally supposed that the design itself had in some way been injured. "Ruined by cleaning" is a common cry in these cases. It is usually sincere, but it may be misled and misleading. A seasoned conservator knows that he can not tell by looking at a picture whether it was in any way damaged by treatment. He can only know that it was damaged. Unless he has at his disposal evidence of its condition before treatment and of the procedures and conditions during treatment, he does not know enough to say whether or not the damage occurred at any particular time.

Unless a picture is stored in a box or sealed away from the air in a frame (Figure 27), it needs some kind of a protective coating, and, in spite of their weakness, varnishes have probably done more good than harm. Better coatings may now be available. New materials that make clear films, capable of being brushed or sprayed, have been developed during the last twenty-five years. These are the so-called "synthetic resins," probably better known as plastics. They are not resins. One of them has had approximately twenty years of continuous use in the treatment of paintings—polymerized vinyl acetate. This is a derivative of vinyl alcohol and is synthesized from acetylene and acetic acid. It is colorless, slightly rubbery, and free from after-yellowing. Other plastics, called "acrylic resins," have come into use more recently. They are polymers of acrylic acid, clear, stable materials best known as molding compounds. Probably other synthetic film substances will be found. On all the evidence available, those now known have a better chance of survival than the natural resins. They have no color, they get less brittle, and in case of damage they can be somewhat more readily removed from the surface of paint.

One other substance which needs to be entered in the list of materials for surface coatings is wax. No single material is perfect as a surface coating, but the history of the use of wax is as long as that of resin or oil, and the record stands strongly in its favor. There may be objections to applying it directly to paint. These have largely to do with appearance—gloss and reflection. For a coating that has stability in itself and protection for the material under it, wax, much the same as that used by the craftsmen of ancient Egypt, is still the best known. Its composition can be varied from the relatively soft beeswax to the very hard carnauba derived from the leaf of a Brazilian palm. As a coating for pictures, the prevalent practice spreads it over a very thin layer of resin or plastic. This gives a certain amount of desired hardness under the wax and it allows the wax to be removed, if it is dusty or scarred, without risk of scratches or wear on the paint itself.

3 · Defects in Paint or Drawing

AMAGE to the construction of a picture is not always accompanied by damage to the paint itself. In complex constructions, where there is a support, a ground, a paint layer, and a surface coating, the paint is held between the ground and the outer surface layer (Figure 2). These other layers take some of the strain and the wear and tear. In simple picture constructions, where the design is laid directly on the support and has no coating over it, small accidents are apt to cause more damage.

Strange things can happen to pictures. Part of a now-famous panel is said to have served awhile as the counter of a fishmonger. Pictures have been hidden, lost, buried, and shipwrecked. War adds to the freaks of their experience, but injury from combat is not yet a major category of defect. Carelessness is the main agent of accidental damage. Paint gets scratched or marked or streaked by drips of water, or splattered by scraps of food or stained by drink. Mold grows in it and insects speckle it. Pictures in the collections of Asia have been kept away from some of these blemishes by being boxed and stored during most of every year. Flies have worked a particular plague on the early, unvarnished pictures of Europe. The excrement of these insects is brown and it is acid. On paint mixed with white it not only leaves a stain but pits the surface by etching away some of the lead carbonate.

Scratches, small dents, or deeper breaks and tears can be recognized by their shape and general appearance (Figure 7 and Plate XI). Glass of a frame broken during shipment is one cause of scratches and may be the cause of deeper damage. Pictures get scratched when they are carried about, dropped, or poorly packed. There is not much that

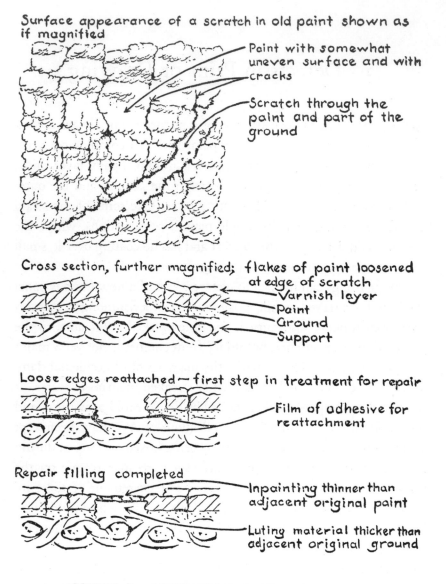

Surface appearance of a scratch in old paint shown as if magnified

Paint with somewhat uneven surface and with cracks

Scratch through the paint and part of the ground

Cross section, further magnified; flakes of paint loosened at edge of scratch
Varnish layer
Paint
Ground
Support

Loose edges reattached — first step in treatment for repair
Film of adhesive for reattachment

Repair filling completed
Inpainting thinner than adjacent original paint
Luting material thicker than adjacent original ground

FIGURE 7 · MECHANICAL DAMAGE TO PAINT
AND THE USUAL REPAIR

can be done about a scratch except to replace the loss. The paint beside the scratch may have been loosened, and in that instance the picture should be put down flat with the face up, in order to prevent the loosened flakes from falling off. Usually they can be reattached. Worm holes are a slight disfigurement to paint on panels (Plate XVII), but the extent of these is not often great, even though the panel may be much damaged. Small, isolated burns such as come from candles do not, as a rule, get into the paint of a varnished picture. The surface coating takes most of the damage, and once that or the paint is injured, not much can be done except to repair the loss. Scorching and the heavy smoke of house fires are more serious, and, short of completely destroying a picture, they can blemish it a great deal, for with a house fire there are extreme heat, fumes, and the action of steam when the fire itself is attacked by water. Added to those is the risk of dousing from a fire extinguisher that throws out a solution of acid. Conditions in a house fire stand as probably the biggest risk of accidental damage to pictures.

The smallest risk of damage probably is the regular accumulation of dust. Those works which are made with paint or pigment directly over fabric or paper are usually covered with glass or are stored in boxes. These containers keep out most of the dirt, but, unless the frame or the box is sealed, small amounts of it work in and collect there. Pictures with varnish and oil paintings in general are usually framed without glass, and the accumulation of dust is inevitable. It often forms in a kind of stubborn crust (Appendix A, 3, and Plates IV and VI). Odd means have been taken to clean it from pictures, and some have probably made the surface more dirty than it was before. One such practice, said to have been followed in the past, was to rub oil—olive oil or a mixture of that with other oils—over the varnish. This produced a temporary gloss which looked well enough but left a sticky film to hold any dust that might settle on it later.

Discoloration of pigment, the granular coloring matter of paint, is a rare occurrence. It does happen with a few pigments and under particular conditions. A small number are inclined to fade when they are exposed to light, particularly in the presence of dampness. Direct sunlight is the strongest fading agent. Ordinary artificial light from a tungsten filament bulb or from lamps or candles is the weakest. Various studies have been made in an effort to discover what part of the spectrum has the greatest influence in changing the color of fugitive pigments. Certain filters and specially prepared glass for frames have been suggested. Few pictures, however, in an ordinary room are exposed to direct sunlight, and there is little occasion to keep them where any strong light needs to be dealt with. The color most likely to fade is a purplish red or maroon, the color of dyes made from madder root, cochineal, the resinous plant product called "dragon's blood," and a few others. In modern painting, coal-tar derivatives in these colors are numerous and may be more fugitive than the traditional dyes drawn from plants and insects. A few, such as alizarin, are more stable. Certain yellow colors and a very few green and orange are also faded by light.

Darkening of pigments is as apt to happen as is fading, and the most common discoloration of this kind is found in drawings where white lead has been used for highlights or high values, or in other works where this same pigment has been exposed to the air. When the white lead has a good amount of binding medium around it or when it is covered with a surface coating, it shows no sign of change even during centuries. The white lead that is not well bound and covered changes to a blackish tone which may have a brown tinge or may have the color of slate. The change is caused by hydrogen sulphide, a gas occurring in small traces in the air of modern cities. This, particularly in dampness, acts on the pigment and converts it from a basic carbonate to a lead sulphide. Red lead, a pigment with a red-orange color, is also darkened under certain circumstances, but the cause is exposure to light, and the best explanation is that light aids in forming a brown lead dioxide from the red tetroxide. This change, like that in the white pigment, happens in pictures where the paint is exposed at the surface, and it has been seen a great deal in the wall paintings of the cave temples of China.

Chemical bleaching is known and is somewhat different from fading. The only common instance of this in pictures is change in the pigment called "ultramarine blue." This is a complicated, inorganic material. It occurs naturally as the semiprecious stone, lapis lazuli, and that, ground to a coarse powder, was much used in Europe until the seventeenth century. Since early in the nineteenth century an artificial ultramarine has been manufactured. This pigment, in either its natural or artificial form, is decomposed even by very weak acids, and complete loss of color results. Such decomposition has been reported in pictures and may have taken place through the formation of acids from decay of organic matter in the picture construction and possibly by something that was accidentally or mistakenly applied.

Probably the most common discoloration of pictures is from the darkening of varnishes. It has been shown how resin or oil-resin films get darker from slow chemical change. This can affect the general color of oil paint, particularly if there is a large amount of oil in the paint mixture, but ordinarily the change is very slight. Parts of an old varnish film are often left on the paint, and these get still darker and more opaque with time and appear as brown spots or streaks lying in hollows of the surface (Figure 8). They can be recognized by this fact, that they are in the low parts of the paint contour. As a rule, they are tough pieces of crust, but they can be removed if time and pains are taken to do it.

Many old paintings, old enough to have had some losses and to have been restored at some time in the past, begin to show a mottled appearance. This spotted discoloration, like the eruption of a skin ailment, is usually seen in the light areas and is not related to the han-

Uneven surface of paint with darkened residues of old
varnish in the depressions; the main part of this former
coating film has been removed.

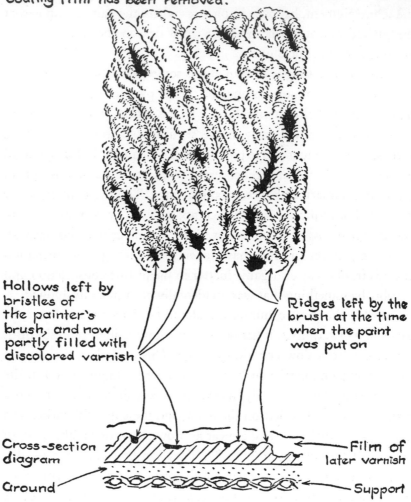

Hollows left by
bristles of
the painter's
brush, and now
partly filled with
discolored varnish

Ridges left by the
brush at the time
when the paint
was put on

Cross-section
diagram

Film of
later varnish

Ground

Support

FIGURE 8 · DISCOLORED VARNISH SPOTS
IN OLD PAINT

dling of the original paint. It may suddenly be noticed if a picture which has hung for years in a dark corner is brought out into full light. When the mottled pattern is studied carefully, it will often show the shapes and the faint contours left by a paint brush (Figure 9 and Plate V). The dark spots are the work of someone called a "restorer" who once made the thing over. He used a fair amount of varnish mixed with the paint, and this caused the patch which once blended with the tones around it to become darker and browner and duller. The aim in painting over these pictures was to make them look new. There was no attempt to keep later paint inside those areas where actual loss had occurred, and often these mottled discolorations amount to ten times the area of the loss.

A common failing in paint exposed to the weather is also a failing of paint which has been sheltered. In the trade this is called "chalking." What happens is that the binding medium, which once went around the pigment particles and held them together in a film, has been broken up and weakened by exposure. Particles of pigment or lumps of such particles then become loosened and fall off. In rain or wind or rough handling of objects, the particles are more apt to fall. Pictures made with pastel crayons or with any soft powder are always open to blemishes because they are chalky from the start. They require great care in framing and handling. The common treatment of paintings on silk or paper in the Far East, where they are unrolled and rolled again at intervals, aggravates any chalking to which weak, thin paint is disposed.

Loss of paint by chalking is sometimes called "skinning," and paint that shows the usual signs of this type of loss is assumed to have been rubbed off. Frequently, also, it is assumed that the loss occurred during a time when varnish was removed from the picture. There is no doubt that abrasion at the surface, any rubbing of the paint itself, is apt to thin a chalky paint (Figure 10 and Plates VI and IX). This could happen during varnish removal and no doubt has happened.

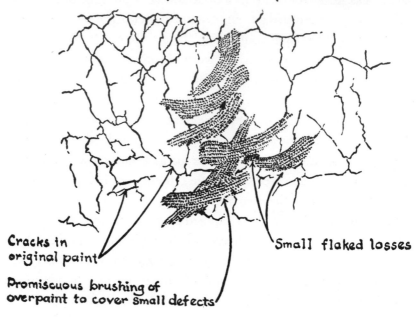

Pattern of darkened overpaint on an old paint surface

Cracks in
original paint

Small flaked losses

Promiscuous brushing of
overpaint to cover small defects

Cross section further enlarged

Discolored overpaint
Small flaked loss

Original paint

Ground

Support

FIGURE 9 · MOTTLED APPEARANCE
CAUSED BY OVERPAINT

Loss along edges of cracks where paint and ground have become cupped

Islands of ground and paint between cracks

Ground exposed where dark paint is rubbed off along edges of cupped islands

Cross section

Exposed ground
Cupped islands
Support

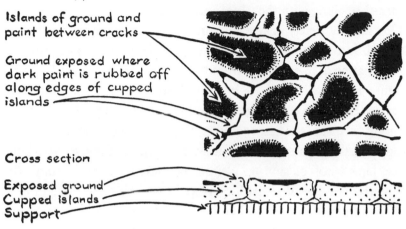

Loss from rubbing of paint over a roughly applied ground such as that sometimes found in Asiatic wall paintings

Ridges caused by rough trowelling or brushing of thin plaster

Smooth ground

Dark paint damaged by rubbing along ridges

Cross section

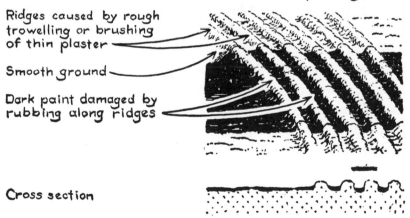

FIGURE 10 · BLEMISHES IN PAINT
FROM RUBBING OR WEARING

Such loss may also have occurred at times when the picture was handled like the rest of the household furniture and was scrubbed and revarnished along with the tables and wainscot.

One kind of defect or loss in paint is, in fact, a kind of chalking, although it may be hard to recognize it in the usual way. This is an actual floating of pigments up from the paint layer into the surface film (Figure 11 and Plate X). It is most likely to be found in the blue areas of European paintings made before 1500. The Italian altar painting furnishes the best example. To get a deep, brilliant blue, the makers of these panel pictures used a pigment of pulverized blue stone, lapis lazuli or azurite. Neither of these is strong in color. By hand processes they were hard to grind finely, and it was thought that the finer they were, the weaker the color became. It is certain that the more adhesive or binding medium put into the paint mixture, the more the color was weakened. The way to get the most out of these pigments was to keep them coarse, use a clear medium like egg white or a glue size, and use as little of that as would hold the particles in place. It is unlikely that any of these pictures was varnished for many years. Varnish would have made the blue look dull and would have spoiled all that the painter had been working for. Before a surface coating was put on, these blue areas had accumulated dirt, and the binding medium in them, being easily affected by dampness and being excellent food for insects, mold, and microorganisms, had often decayed. In these areas the pigment particles lay together like dust. When varnish was put on, this dust was carried up into the film of the new coating, and from that time on the color of the blue could not be recovered (Figure 11). Varnish soaked down also into the absorbent paint below. After a few decades of decomposition in the varnish film, the blue paint is nearly black and may have a greenish tinge.

The sign of chalking is an over-all thinning of the paint, often with exposure of the ground or support underneath. Chalked paint needs

Diagram of chalky paint in magnified cross section

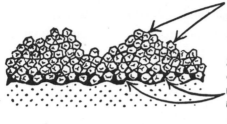

Loose pigment particles in upper part of paint layer

Shown as dark, small amounts of binding medium hold pigment particles in lower part of paint layer

Magnified cross section of chalky paint after it has been coated with a film material such as varnish

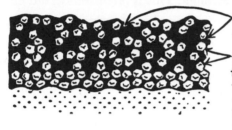

Heavy layer of coating

Pigment particles floated up at the time of application and now held in the dried coating film.

Varnish put over a chalky paint becomes the binding medium of the loose pigment. The color of the pigment is offset by the color of the varnish which tends to get dark and brown with age.

FIGURE II · FLOATING OF CHALKY PAINT

to be distinguished from paint that is put on thinly (Figure 12). If paint has been originally applied in a very thin layer, it will show the marking or streaking of the brush or tool which spread it. Chalked paint lacks any such mark and is usually uneven in a pattern of wear rather than in a pattern related to the design.

A defect of paint which may be confused with chalking or thinning is *pentimento*. This carries with it no loss of pigment or medium. Theoretically the cause is a progressive change of refractive index in an oil medium. Such a change is known to occur in a drying oil. The index of refraction rises, and more light goes through the paint layer. It becomes more translucent. Drawing and underpaint which it once covered begin to show through. This is often seen in old oil pictures. What is seen may come from a number of causes—wearing and chalking as well as a rising index of refraction.

A common mark of old paint is the set of cracks that form in it. Cracks are seen in paint which has enough binding medium to stand as a separate film. It tends to become brittle rather than chalky with age. There is no way to prevent this entirely in the mixture of the paint itself, for a film which has so little medium that it will not crack under any circumstances is a film too weak and porous to stand the normal conditions of exposure which pictures have to take. Such a paint, as has just been noticed, is easily scarred and must be especially framed and handled. It catches dust, grime, and stain which can not be removed from it.

The kind of binding medium in the paint probably has some influence on the kind of cracks that are formed. There are those who say that they can distinguish a tempera or aqueous paint from an oil paint by the different patterns of the cracks in the two, and that there is a crackle or crack system peculiar to paint that has an emulsion medium. Evidence for such judgments has not been brought out or clarified. Factors other than the nature of the medium probably have a great deal to do with the formation of cracks in paint: the way in

Area of chalked paint

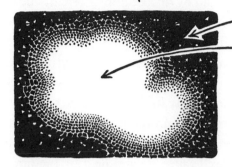

Dark paint moderately thick

Ground exposed where dark paint has fallen off as a result of chalking

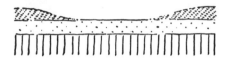

Cross section

Paint thinly applied

Heavy paint of light color

Ground exposed in fine streaks where brush was drawn through thin dark paint

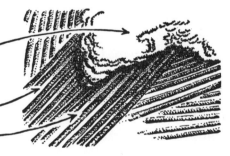

Cross section

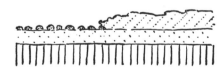

FIGURE 12 · CHALKED PAINT COMPARED
WITH THINLY APPLIED PAINT

which different layers were put on, the relative drying rates, the thickness of part of the paint layer and of the aggregate of paint and ground, and the strains caused by support and by surface film. There has never been discovered a binding medium which will stay flexible and also will get hard enough to serve its primary purpose of holding pigments securely in place. Brittleness seems sure to develop in paint of any considerable body. When such paint gets brittle, it will crack along the lines of its own weakness if any strain is put on it.

Without much doubt, the greatest strain put upon paint is by the support under it. Thin pictures on paper or on fabric have so little medium and have the paint so well taken up and held by the fibers of the support that cracks are not a common ailment of drawings, water colors, or the scroll paintings of Asia. In a sense, these are stained or colored supports, and the paint layer has no independence. The traditional picture of the Western world has a moderately thick paint, usually on a smooth ground coat, laid over wood or fabric. This type of paint and ground construction is subject to cracking. Of the two supports, wood seems to have caused more trouble in this way than fabric. It is used in its natural state. The whole arrangement of its cell structure remains after it is cut and dried. The system which gave the means of life to a tree stands as a means of moisture transmission and as a cause of instability. When the air is damp, the wood swells, and when the air is dry, the wood shrinks. While the paint and ground are still flexible, they are able to move with these changes of the weather, but as they get old and stiff, they can not take this continual disturbance. And so they crack. In appearance this type of crack is thin and fine. It runs in lines which may cross over in a net or branch out in an irregular way (Figure 13). In smaller measure, canvas or fabric has somewhat the same action as wood on an old and brittle film of paint. This action is aggravated by the usual treatment of the fabric. Untreated linen or other cloth will go slack as it gets dry and tighten when it is damp; the larger the picture, the more noticeable the slack-

Four typical patterns—details from paintings; the number of pattern types is large and they show wide variations in the size of the interval between cracks

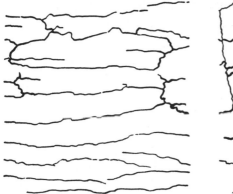

Panel painting, fourteenth century

Panel painting, fourteenth century

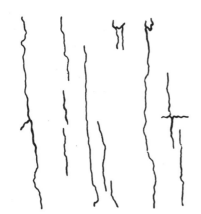

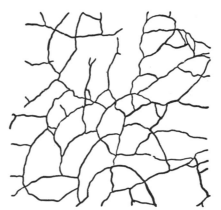

Panel painting, fifteenth century

Painting on canvas, seventeenth century

FIGURE 13 · CRACKS IN PAINT AND GROUND
CAUSED BY STRAIN FROM MOVEMENT
OF THE SUPPORT

ening becomes. But the extent of this movement is not great. What causes the most strain on the paint is sizing material, usually glue, put into the fabric while it is being prepared for painting and, in the old days, multiplied in volume by relining or rebacking with a great amount of glue adhesive. The glue swells and makes the fabric go slack in dampness; it tightens when it is dry, and its response is much greater by volume and much quicker in time than that of the fabric alone.

Another kind of cracking which some paint shows is caused not by strain from the outside but by stresses within the paint itself. Anyone who has studied scientifically the oil paint of modern art and modern industry will know that the coating takes a long time to dry. Ultimately the dried film is smaller in volume than the wet film that was applied. The length of time is influenced by a number of conditions. Different pigments cause oil to dry at different rates. Certain organometallic compounds called "driers," put into the paint, cut down the drying time. The kind of oil and the solvent or diluent used with it make some difference. If oil is to be used reasonably in picture-making, some understanding must be reached of the natural processes which go on in the drying and aging of oil paint. Without such understanding, construction is likely to be poor. Many a pretentious picture begins to crack within weeks after it is finished. It cracks before any strain from the outside could have affected it. This happens because quick-drying layers are put over soft and slow-drying paint. When the quick-drying layers begin to shrink, they slide over the spongy mass beneath and rupture themselves in the process (Figure 14). Cracks of this kind are often seen in glazed areas thick with medium and sparse in pigment. They appear where the painter has failed to let a coating dry before adding the next one or where he has made a still more headstrong effort to run against natural forces and has put a retouching varnish over a soft paint so that he could work over it.

Breaks in the paint layer caused by failure of the film to withstand the strain of its own contraction during the drying process.

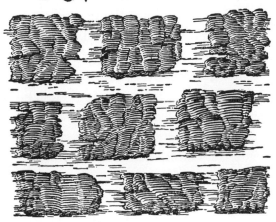

Paint applied over an unstable film like bitumen and covered over with a thick layer of varnish often splits open into wide rifts from the pull of drying. This has been called "alligator crackle" or "alligatoring."

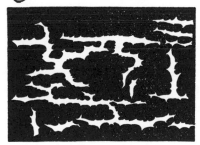 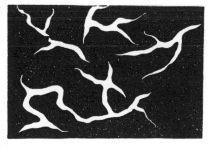

Two patterns of cracks out of many that may develop in paint which shrinks more on the top surface than in the under part of the film.

FIGURE 14 · SHRINKAGE CRACKS IN PAINT

A great deal has been said about the influence of bitumen or asphaltum pigment in causing cracks. There is not much laboratory evidence on it. Certain comments concerning bitumen were made in writings of the eighteenth and nineteenth centuries, and it can still be bought. It has a dark, brownish-neutral color and seems to have been used mainly to tone down dark areas of oil pictures. The pigment usually contains certain hydrocarbons that remain soft. And it fuses with oil and keeps that from getting thoroughly dry. Left entirely alone, the oil film with bitumen in it may be stable. Experiments with it show that over a period of twenty years the film has not changed. When a paint which can form a hard film is put over it, however, that upper film pulls, crawls, and cracks because it lacks a firm grip on any surface beneath it. The soft layer of paint is pulled with it. Such films have been seen to open in crevices as much as a quarter inch across (Figure 14). A wide aperture is a characteristic of all cracks caused by the inability of a paint film to hold together while it dries. As the aperture is wide, the paint between the cracks is apt to be lumpy, pulled up in a kind of blob. The edge of the crack has a fluid appearance like the bank of a muddy river. It is different from the thin, fractured edge, like that of broken glass, seen in paint that has cracked because of strain from outside.

Spots of one kind or another appear on pictures from a variety of causes, and some comment has already been made on a few of these —defects in the varnish and discoloration of old overpainting among them. Spots are also caused by mold, and there are few kinds of pictures which will not grow mold if they are given a good chance. More subject to it are the pictures on paper or on cloth which are painted with some kind of water color and have no surface coating. Drawings come into this, as do most of the portable paintings of the Far East, the works on silk and on paper, water color paintings of the kind done in the West during the last hundred and fifty years, and the chalk pictures known as pastels. These are most inclined to get moldy. For one reason, they are often stored over long periods in places that get damp. For another, they contain good food for the varieties of plant life known as mold. All that these plants need is moisture, oxygen, and protein. The moisture must be fairly high, but no higher than a cool cellar would afford during most of the summer or than any room would have at certain times in sultry weather. Thin, simple constructions are most susceptible, but heavy oil paint and varnished pictures often get moldy. Resin varnish or wax is not apt to be infested, but canvas, especially when sized or relined with glue, is as good a bed for the growth of these plants as can be found, and the plants can work their way from the back into the paint layer (Figure 15 and Plates VII and VIII).

The appearance of mold does not need to be described in detail. Everyone has seen it, and the mold that grows on pictures is no different from the mold that grows on other things. The air is full of these common spores, and most surfaces that are not constantly scrubbed are apt to hold them. The growth may be noticed as light or dark spots, masses of the stems of the plants, and with a good magnifying glass the stems themselves can be seen. In oil paintings mold spots are likely to appear first along the cracks, but by that time the back of the canvas will usually be found to have a heavy growth. Mold feeds on the materials in the pictures that it infests, and some part of these materials is naturally destroyed. Paint gets pitted or otherwise marked. Ground and support are weakened. There may be a good deal of staining, particularly of paper or fabric. Most of the plants die among the fibers or in the paint, and the residue or its decomposition causes spots and stains.

Many of the defects that come with damage to paint and drawing can not be corrected, and most of those which can in any way be improved by treatment need to be handled by professional conservators.

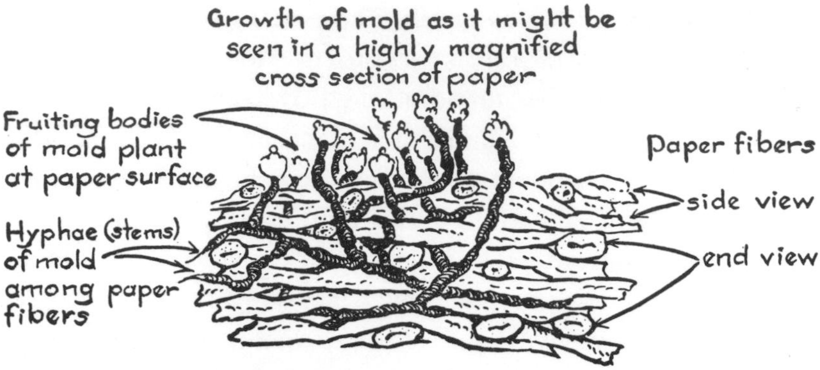

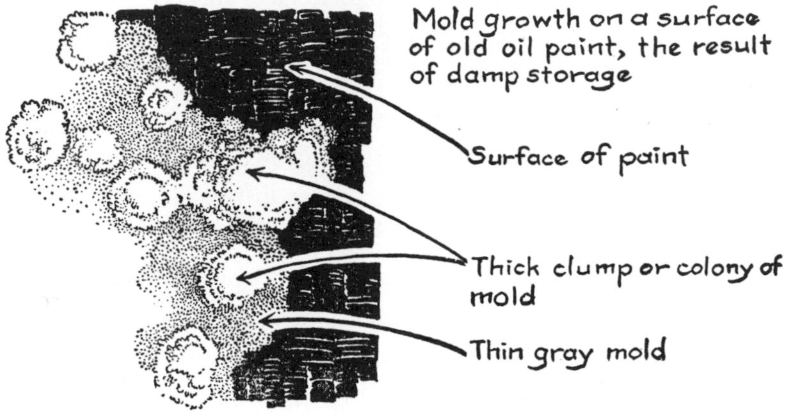

Growth of mold as it might be
seen in a highly magnified
cross section of paper

Fruiting bodies
of mold plant
at paper surface

Paper fibers

side view

end view

Hyphae (stems)
of mold
among paper
fibers

Mold growth on a surface
of old oil paint, the result
of damp storage

Surface of paint

Thick clump or colony of
mold

Thin gray mold

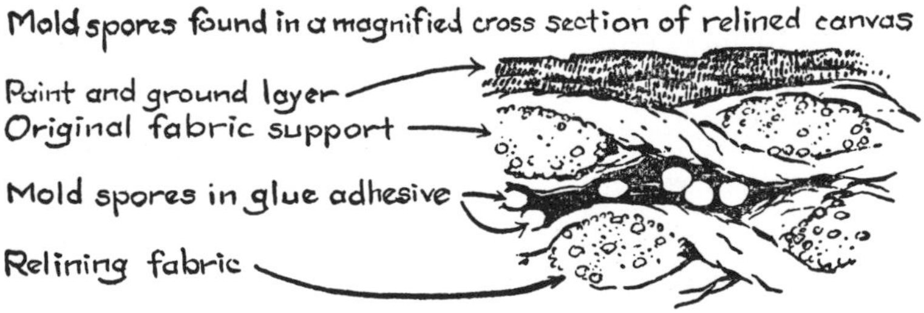

Mold spores found in a magnified cross section of relined canvas

Paint and ground layer
Original fabric support

Mold spores in glue adhesive

Relining fabric

FIGURE 15 · MOLD IN PICTURE MATERIALS

No sound way is known to repair or obliterate paint cracks. These are normal marks of age or inescapable shortcomings in construction, and general agreement is to leave them alone.

Breaks, scratches, or scars can be helped somewhat by reattachment of the edges and by appropriate inpainting of the lost areas (Figures 7 and 16 and Plate XII). A great deal has been said about this among museum administrators and curators, dealers, connoisseurs, and art historians. Some take the view that a damaged picture can not be improved. Fifteen or twenty years ago certain European scholars argued that way. One of them wrote:

In his eyes [the eyes of the scholar], every restoration which goes beyond cleaning, preserving, and uncovering is a piece of counterfeiting—whether successful or not. Indeed, logically he must regard the skillful and consequently deceptive repair as more damaging and dangerous than the unsuccessful and therefore easily recognizable. He wants to see as much as has been preserved of what the artist created, and he revolts against being left in uncertainty regarding that which is lacking.*

In words the argument looks all right, but in practice not many scholars who are responsible for collections of pictures have acted on it. They are probably put off by the confusion and distraction of holes having various shapes, colors, and values, and probably by advice that the edges of these holes in the paint are apt to work loose and be snagged and further torn.

The usual procedure is to fill the losses. A good deal of defacement has been done in the foolish attempt to cover up all signs of loss (Appendix A, 2, and Plate XIII). In the past, some painter-restorers got into their heads the conviction that they could work in the same way as the artists whose damaged pictures they had to repair, and they went over the whole areas to make them look new. This, of course, was nonsense. But a moderate compensation of loss where that loss

* Max J. Friedländer, *Genuine and Counterfeit,* tr. by Carl Von Honstett and Lenore Pelham (New York, Boni, 1930), p. 28.

Area of loss where chip of paint, with part of ground layer, has flaked out

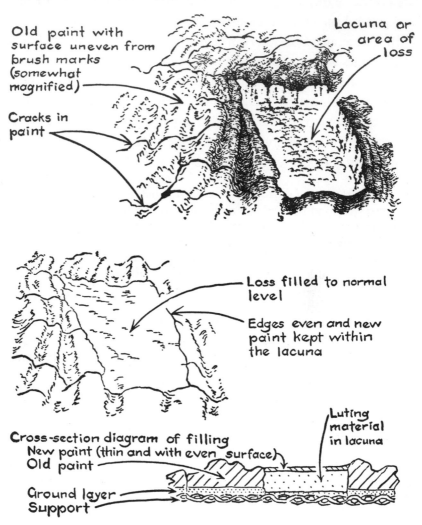

Old paint with surface uneven from brush marks (somewhat magnified)

Lacuna or area of loss

Cracks in paint

Loss filled to normal level

Edges even and new paint kept within the lacuna

Luting material in lacuna

Cross-section diagram of filling
New paint (thin and with even surface)
Old paint

Ground layer
Support

FIGURE 16 · FILLING OF PAINT LOSS

is a distinct blemish to a design can usually be made without stepping over the boundaries. Each case sets its own problem.

Old overpaint causing mottled tones can usually be removed from the original paint (Appendix A, 2), and a certain amount of stain and grime also can be removed (Appendix A, 3, and Plate IV). It is useless, however, to speak about taking off any kind of discoloration from a picture as if rules could be laid down for such procedure and could be safely followed by anyone who has not had professional training. There is no doubt that pictures have been cleaned by untrained persons, washed with soap and water, brushed with oil, wiped with slices of potato or of onion, or with bread dough, and have suffered no apparent loss. Some pictures can take it. But not all. Only a trained person can tell by technical examination exactly what a certain paint construction is able to stand.

In such a technical examination, the picture is looked over for its general appearance, for the earmarks of material, the kind of support it has, the thickness of ground, the markings in the paint, the distribution, tone, and type of discoloration. It is studied microscopically over the surface, and then the reactions of the different layers are tested with a range of solvents. The number of these solvents that might be used is in the hundreds. The number that is ordinarily used is not more than a score, but the items that make up that number are combined with each other on the basis of experience to produce a certain speed of solvent action and rate of drying which will be suitable to the procedure of film or grime removal. In difficult cases the nature of the binding medium in the original paint and in the ground is studied by microchemical analysis. When all of this has been done, a plan for the removal is devised, the materials and tools are brought together, and the work starts (Appendix A, 1–4). It may not go according to the original plan. Factors of timing, temperature, and manipulation are part of it. Without experience and without standard laboratory equipment and controls, removal of encrusted substances from the surface of a picture is not safe.

Except for the needs of special treatment, most pictures can be conditioned for a normal housing and can be taken care of in a routine way like other objects in a room. First, however, it must be certain that they can be treated in this way, and it must be certain what amount of moving, handling, and housecleaning they will take without risk of damage. Anyone trained in conservation can supply the answers in doubtful cases. In many cases anyone with common sense can see the answers. A picture made with pastels obviously can not be gone over with a feather duster unless the picture is properly framed (Figure 27). Well sealed in a tight frame with glass, it can stand dusting, but under the best of circumstances it is in a poor way to stand much moving or transportation. The coloring is loose like powder, and jolting tends to dislodge it.

Discoloration of pigment itself usually can not be repaired. A dye color which has lost its intensity because of fading has lost it for good. The darkening of red lead has as yet no means of correction, nor has the bleaching out of ultramarine blue. Darkened white lead can, however, be restored to its original tone. The change from white to a blackish gray or brown is a change from a carbonate to a sulphide in the lead salt. But another lead compound, the sulphate, is white, and the sulphide can be changed into the white sulphate by application of hydrogen peroxide. It takes a certain technique to make this application, but when it is done, as it often is done on European drawings, the color is recovered.

If all pictures could be kept in air-conditioned, shockproof rooms with constant temperature and relative humidity, many of the ailments reviewed here would not develop. Materials would still oxidize and varnish would get darker, but deterioration of the other organic materials—the binding mediums, the wood and paper and fabric— would be slowed down to a pace that was negligible. A great deal of the deterioration in these organic materials comes from insects and from mold and microorganisms. Mold, in particular, will not grow unless the relative humidity in a room exceeds 60 percent during a long period and usually 70 percent for a shorter period. There are not many houses where pictures are kept that can hold relative humidity below the 60 percent level throughout the year. Accommodation to usual conditions of housing and measures to prevent the growth of mold will be taken up later. Something can be said here, however, about the treatment of pictures in which mold growth has already started.

Where the mold is heavy and the picture is weak or fragile—a drawing, a water color, a miniature, a silk or paper scroll, or a pastel (Plate VII)—about all that can be done is to get it dry. This will stop the growth. A conservator will have to do what he can from that point on. If the growth is slight and the picture is strong—a varnished canvas or panel—it may be handled without professional aid. First it must be dried in a normally dry room with normal light and temperature. When the picture is dry, the mold is brushed off with a soft brush. Then the picture is fumigated by being put in a dry, tight box containing loose crystals of thymol or paradichlorobenzene. A frame is made which will seal the picture (Figure 27). It is put into the frame and with it, at the back, is put a strip of cloth or blotting paper dampened with an alcoholic solution of paradichlorobenzene or thymol.

4 · Ground: Weakness and Damage

THAT layer of the picture which is called "ground" is probably not much known or much thought about in the general care of pictures. It occurs only in complex constructions. Unless there is a good deal of damage to the paint, the ground is never seen. From the front it lies buried under paint and varnish and from the back it is hidden by the support. In spite of its obscurity, this ground layer is a frequent cause of a great amount of trouble. The least of its troubles are stains, discolorations, and scars, the defects that are most easily noticed in paint. They are found in the ground layer but do not often cause any conspicuous disfigurement to the design (Figure 17 and Plate X). Any scratch or other mutilation which reaches the ground has already caused greater damage to the paint. Brown splotches from oils or resins soaked through the paint appear only if the paint itself is worn thin, and the speckled areas caused by mold are apt to be more noticeable in the design layer than in the smooth coat underneath it.

Most of the cracks seen in paint—fine linear or network patterns of breaks usual in old pictures—ordinarily extend up into the paint from the ground (Figures 13 and 17). There are panel paintings that have a double system of cracks, one inside the other. The smaller of these is regularly in the paint and the larger in the ground and paint together. The shrinkage cracks already spoken about (Figure 14), caused by failure of the paint to stand the strain of its own contraction when it dries, do not get into the ground. Both of these are unusual. Most of the cracks or crackle patterns that are seen start in the ground near the plane where it is laid on the support and run up like thin crevices through the paint and often through the varnish.

Diagrams of highly magnified cross sections of complex painting construction

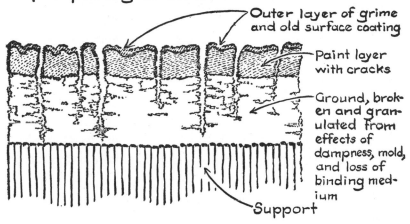

Outer layer of grime and old surface coating

Paint layer with cracks

Ground, broken and granulated from effects of dampness, mold, and loss of binding medium

Support

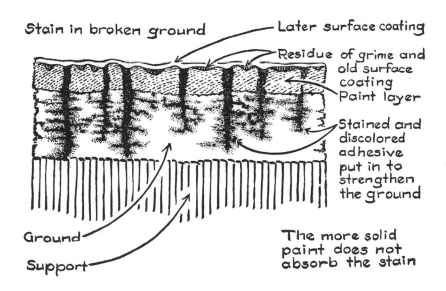

Stain in broken ground

Later surface coating

Residue of grime and old surface coating

Paint layer

Stained and discolored adhesive put in to strengthen the ground

Ground

Support

The more solid paint does not absorb the stain

FIGURE 17 · BROKEN AND STAINED GROUND

The main cause of cracks in the ground is also the cause of disruption, of loosening or cleavage, of loss of the original paint, and is probably the greatest single cause of damage to pictures. It needs to be rationally comprehended and constantly kept in mind. Fundamentally, the source of this damage lies in the incompatibility between ground and support. As materials these are far apart, and as constructions they are extremely different. For pictures which have grounds the common supports are wood and fabric. The ground is a kind of loosely bound paint. It is usually bound by glue or oil. In any case it is an organic substance, lying, in a more or less hardened film, in and among the grains of an inert substance. The organic binding material is undergoing progressive deterioration. It is constantly losing its adhesive strength, its tensile strength as a film substance, and its flexibility. Mixed with it are the granules of an inert substance comparable to the pigment in paint. The old inert filler of grounds, adopted in the eastern Mediterranean region during ancient times, used in the icons of Byzantium and Greece, and standard in the panel paintings of Italy, was gypsum. This is a calcium sulphate dihydrate, laid down as a deposit in many parts of the world. When the water of crystallization is driven off by heat, gypsum serves as a setting cement and is now known as plaster of Paris. To some extent it may have been used unburnt and pulverized when taken for an inert substance in panel grounds. It is stable but is slightly soluble in water. It makes a firm, hard layer when mixed with glue and allowed to dry. The other traditional inert filler was chalk or whiting. This was used in the north of Europe, where there were ample deposits of it. It is a more or less white powder, a natural calcium carbonate made up, to a large extent, of the remains of minute sea organisms. White lead seems to have come into use only in recent centuries as an inert filler in oil grounds.

The film character or structure of grounds is normally lean; there is a small amount of medium in proportion to the inert substance

(Figure 3). When the picture was made, this was a practical necessity. The ground had to be chalky so that it could be scraped and abraded to a smooth surface. It had to take charcoal for preliminary drawing, and it had to take paint easily. It is a stiff and brittle layer. And it lies like a thin, weak crust against a fibrous mass that is tough, active, and restless. The wood or fabric shrinks, swells, and twists in the changing air around it. A very few picturemakers were smart enough to put grounds on both sides of a panel and to put a coat of paint on the back. Pictures have kept better when they were treated that way, and a coating at the back, applied to an old support, will help to stabilize it. But no such coating can entirely stop its movement. The outcome is easy to predict. The support tends to shear itself from the brittle layer put on it (Figure 18). If that layer breaks in time and breaks at right angles to the face of the support, it may be able to accommodate itself to the movement underneath. The lines of the breaks are open cracks that run among small islands of the ground. These can keep a hold on the support far better than the unbroken crust of the ground. The changes in the support are taken up by the cracks. The ground, with the paint over it, is like a mass of scales.

Often the island, the irregular flake cut off by cracks on all sides, takes on the shape of a saucer. The edges are curved upward (Figure 18). At these buckled edges the ground is usually loosened from a wooden support. An aqueous ground, one that is bound with glue, may have swollen at the edges of the islands from dampness condensed in the cracks. Loss of paint from abrasion, as has been described earlier, is greatest around the buckled edges of these concave islands. On a fabric support the curled edges may not have been loosened. If the fabric is thin, it will often stick with the ground and show grooves or creases at the back corresponding to the ridges at the front (Plate XV).

Over a number of years a wood panel loses a fraction of its width across the grain. Even though it is kept in a humid atmosphere, it

Separation of ground layer from support occurs usually in pictures on panel

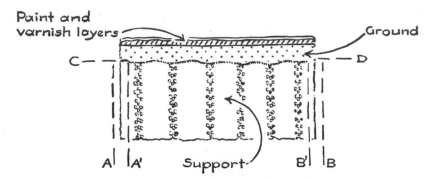

Paint and
varnish layers

Ground

C — — — — — — — — D

A' A'   Support   B' B

The wood of the support moves laterally with changes in moisture content. When damp it will swell to AB; when dry it will shrink to A'B'. Failure of the increasingly brittle ground to move with the support tends to break it loose along the line CD.

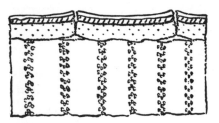

Weakened by deterioration of medium and by strain, the ground cracks, is broken loose near the cracks, and is pushed slightly away from the support (buckling)

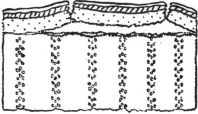

Further movement in the support loosens flakes of ground; these may stay in place because they are caught at the edges (cleavage)

FIGURE 18 · DEVELOPMENT OF CLEAVAGE

does not often swell to its original span. This means that all of the ground on such a support is compressed laterally and tends to be pushed up. The edges of concave, buckled islands strike each other and, when the panel shrinks to its smallest size in a dry place, some of the islands or flakes may finally get loosened in the center and the cleavage of such flakes is complete (Figure 18). If this is only one flake, it probably will stay in place because it is lodged and bonded at the edges. That is enough to hold it against any usual strain, but an unusual or sharp strain such as a hard blow, or long vibration during transport, would knock it out. When a loosened flake is adjacent to a number of others that are loose also and when cleavage extends to a larger area, pieces are apt to fall out because of some casual disturbance—handling, building vibration, or even a draft of air in the room.

Cleavage of ground from the support is less common in pictures on fabric, but it does occur. Although the cause has a slightly different explanation, it is substantially the same. Ordinary observation of the behavior of these supports brings out what seems to be a contradiction. Fabrics, in common experience, draw up taut when they are wet and go slack when dry. The canvas of pictures does the opposite. A period of damp weather will make a large picture sag and bulge on its stretcher. The difference, apparently, is in the glue sizing or glue re-lining of the fabric. Gelatin, soaked through the threads, is softened and swollen by dampness, and its response overrides that of the fiber. Cleavage of ground occurs also in pictures done on metal or stone. These supports are not affected by changes of dampness in the air. Temperature has a slight influence on the dimensions but hardly enough to unseat a ground or paint that was normally well attached. Cleavage, buckling, and loss by flaking from these more stable supports bring into view a second or subordinate cause of all such loosening of the ground. This is the embrittling effect and the strain on paint and ground that come from the surface coating. Ground and paint themselves tend to get more brittle, but this tendency does not go so far in gelatin or oil as it goes in a resin. It is held back, also, by the pigment particles and the inert substances which make up the bulk of these layers. The granules block shrinkage and keep it small. In surface coatings there is nothing to relieve the extreme brittleness that comes with long drying and oxidation and nothing much to stop the shrinkage of a varnish layer. This layer is stuck to the paint under-neath and the paint, in turn, to the ground. As the outer varnish pulls itself into a broken and curled crust, it naturally tends to pull the under structures with it (Appendix A, 6, and Plate XVI).

A picture can have cleavage and give no clear sign at the surface that it is there, but the breakup or separation of layers in the construc-tion is very unusual without some slight change of plane that becomes visible on the surface (Figure 19). The change may be so small that it can be detected only with the help of special lighting. One such means is so-called "raking" light, a beam thrown across the surface and almost in the plane of it. This picks up minute differences of con-tour the way a low sun illuminates contours on the earth (Plates XIV and XV). Differences of this kind also can be seen if the surface is shiny and is viewed in the angle of reflection (Figure 4), that is, with the eye of the observer catching the light that is reflected by the surface from the light source. The more evident sign of cleavage, so-called "buckling," in which the ground and upper layers are pushed up along the edges of cracks, is not hard to recognize.

The problem of repair for cleavage and buckling is a much tougher problem than is usually supposed. Glib talk is often heard on this sub-ject, for it is easy to say that all a picture needs is to have some loose paint set down, some "blisters" taken care of. Actually, it is quite a job. As a rule, it is not very difficult to get the paint flat again, and a great many operators have trapped themselves into believing that because it was flat it was entirely reattached. Such pictures come back for an-other repair treatment in a few years. The repeated application of adhesives from one workshop or laboratory to another is not the best

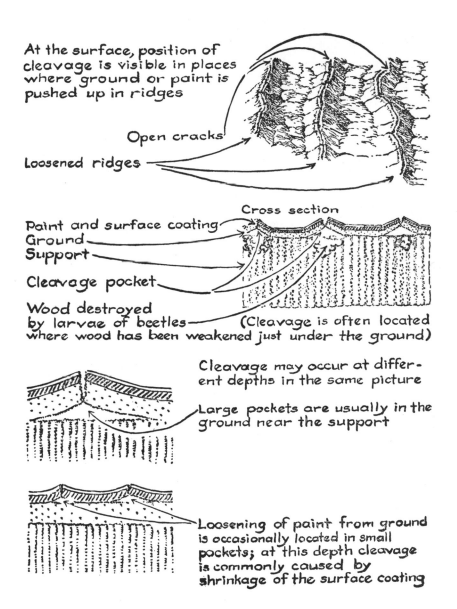

At the surface, position of cleavage is visible in places where ground or paint is pushed up in ridges

Open cracks

Loosened ridges

Cross section

Paint and surface coating
Ground
Support

Cleavage pocket

Wood destroyed by larvae of beetles

(Cleavage is often located where wood has been weakened just under the ground)

Cleavage may occur at different depths in the same picture

Large pockets are usually in the ground near the support

Loosening of paint from ground is occasionally located in small pockets; at this depth cleavage is commonly caused by shrinkage of the surface coating

FIGURE 19 · LOCATION OF CLEAVAGE
IN POSITION AND IN DEPTH

that could be done for the conservation of these works. Complete re-attachment can occasionally be carried out without disturbances to any of the existing layers in the picture construction. Often, however, the surface coating is so brittle and has so strong a hold on the films underneath it that this top film must come off. In some instances local re-attachment can not possibly be effected, and there are those cases in which the cleavage has been so general and access to the cleavage level so poor through the paint that the entire ground must be transferred to another support.

Mainly, the types of repair treatment, short of transfer, are all much alike. The reason for the cleavage is original lack or later loss of adhesive or binding medium in the layer where that cleavage occurs. By some means an adhesive has to be put where it is needed, to be infused or injected or otherwise introduced into the pocket of separation. In some cases the buckling is open enough to provide access from the surface (Figure 20 and Appendix A, 6). Where there is no access through cracks and openings that are naturally caused, conservators in the past have followed the practice of putting holes in the paint cracks to afford such access. This could be done in a tidy way, but often it was not and sound paint was defaced by holes and later painted over. The difficulty with any infusion process is to get the adhesive that is applied to travel any distance into the cleavage pocket. This is, at best, a blind procedure. If the amount of adhesive is too slight, the defect is not remedied. If it is too great, the paint and ground are likely to be made brittle by it, and they will curl and buckle at a later time. Another method is to swing up the loosened ground on a facing like a hinge (Figure 20) and to put the adhesive in the pocket by direct brushing. This is somewhat more efficient but carries other risks. Weak adhesion of the facing may let paint or ground particles get out of line. Edges of flakes are apt to be chipped as the pieces are moved in and out of position. If there is cleavage at different levels in the paint-ground complex, portions may fall apart

Unless the support is too weak to be kept, loose ground is reattached and the whole construction is given a seal against moisture

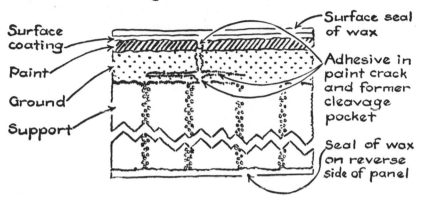

Surface coating

Paint

Ground

Support

Surface seal of wax

Adhesive in paint crack and former cleavage pocket

Seal of wax on reverse side of panel

Hinged reattachment: Where adhesive can not be infused directly into cleavage pockets, loose flakes are occasionally swung up on a tight facing and set down with adhesive put on opened surfaces

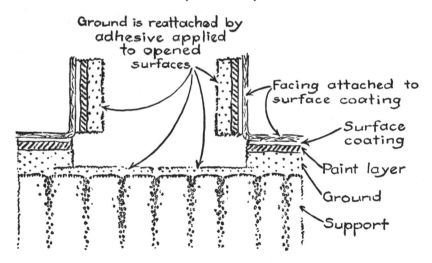

Ground is reattached by adhesive applied to opened surfaces

Facing attached to surface coating

Surface coating

Paint layer

Ground

Support

FIGURE 20 · TREATMENT OF CLEAVAGE

and complete control of the fragments will be lost. These risks are considerable. In view of all the difficulties, it must be evident that easy comments on this type of treatment are backed up by a very slight knowledge of the problem. A seasoned conservator has to take a careful assessment of cleavage before he starts to work on it. He must calculate the adhesive or adhesives to be used and figure out their proper concentrations. In the end he will know that he has improved a condition, but he will probably know, also, that he has not corrected it and that he or someone has a good chance to see part of it again (Appendix A, 5).

Cleavage must be treated by a professional, but certain general precautions concerning pictures that have loose paint may be a convenience for anyone who is responsible for such objects. The safe procedure is to take down from the wall a picture, particularly one on a panel support, when it shows definite buckling. The work should then be stored flat and face up so that gravity holds the loose flakes in place. An impulse to touch the buckled spot has to be overcome. Giving in to natural curiosity about how it feels may shatter the flake; a sound rule is hands off. In a flat position the picture can be moved short distances if it is carefully held, but it can not be packed or shipped with safety. Prior to any packing the buckled areas need to be faced, and that is necessarily the beginning of the treatment and should be the work of a trained conservator.

5 · Flaws in the Support

MANY of the old shops where pictures were treated and where the treatment went by the name of restoration often divided their labor. The man who worked on the paint and the ground had nothing to do with the material underneath it. He may not even have looked at the condition of the support. The man who worked on the support often did not see the paint at all because the picture came to him with a paper pasted over the entire front. For this man the care of the support was a kind of cabinetmaking job. It was his business to make a piece of wood or a piece of fabric as strong as he could. It probably never occurred to the good workmen in these shops that a support could be too strong for the paint. Apparently it did not occur to anyone in the practice of picture repair that the only value of a support in a complex construction was to carry a piece of design in paint and that anything done to the material underneath the ground and the paint would have some effect on the state and the character of the design.

Since nobody thought of this, it was natural to look at the support as something to be treated by itself. In the long run, these traditional materials, wood and fabric particularly, which ought to provide a firm and lasting base for paint, are subject to more damage, more varied and more active damage, than the paint itself. They are stronger at the start, but with time and with the usual conditions of exposure they weaken or they behave badly. They show a range of flaws—cracks, breaks or tears, warping, wrinkling, or other distortion, worm holes, stains, and rot. A careful look at all sides of the picture will take in easily most of these flaws. They can be watched for in the order of the damage to the support, from complete loss of material down to slight distortions or discolorations.

Many a picture has lost part of its support and usually part of the design with it. As a rule, this happens at the edges. It may show plainly in the composition of a picture or it may be certain only from marks in the support itself. If a fabric has a tacking margin beyond the paint on all sides but one, that one may well have been cut. If a panel has the marks of a plane on only one side and if the worm tunnels are laid open at these marks, that side has been cut. A large number of such losses has occurred. The support may have been badly damaged along one side or have had a loss at a corner. Cutting away part was the laziest and the cheapest way to get out of a tedious repair. A few pictures have had pieces added to them. The aim seems to have been to make the thing fit a frame that was handy. If the support, the actual original support and not some later addition, can be seen, smaller types of loss are apt to be found in old pictures. They will be repaired and painted over at the front. Knot holes in wood may be plugged or filled. A fabric may have a new corner. Holes in paper are often found patched with an inset piece. Such losses are a nuisance (a flaw is always bothersome), but they will not get worse and, unless they have led to wide overpainting in adjacent areas, nothing much can be done about them.

The flaw to look for is the kind that may get worse or may be a disturbance to the ground and the paint. In those rare supports which are stone or metal or glass, cracks or breaks are a passive sort of defect. The thing has been injured and that is that. It may have to be repaired in order to allow for safe handling or to give a work better appearance, but, like complete losses, once done they will get no worse of themselves. A crack in wood is another matter. Even a small check is a sign that something has gone wrong. The wood can not adjust itself to some strain in its own structure or strain caused by an attachment on it. A tear in paper or in parchment may occur because the edges are stuck down and the sheet is pulling against adhesion to a mount. That can go on and cause more damage. These are kinds of defects that need to be watched for—the ones that can not be explained by accident or unusual handling.

Distortion of a support may also be a sign that it is under some strain, and further damage may come of that. With rare exceptions, pictures are made on flat surfaces, and a good deal of trouble is taken and has been taken in the past to get these surfaces flat and smooth. If they are twisted out of shape, they confuse the design that is on them and can be somewhat weakened by it themselves. Paper and parchment probably have been distorted more than other supports because they get creased and folded (Appendix A, 10, and Plate XVIII). Rolling does somewhat less harm. Inventors of fiction are fond of having a great masterpiece cut out of its frame, twisted into a tight roll, and carried in an umbrella. Except in these stories, few European or American paintings have ever been rolled. Large pictures may have to be handled that way in extreme circumstances. During 1940 the big canvas by Rembrandt called "The Night Watch" was removed from the Rijksmuseum in Amsterdam and eventually rested, rolled on a cylinder, in a repository near Maastricht. When such a measure is needed, a large cylinder or drum is used. More than 90 percent of the movable paintings of the Far East, however, have been or are kept rolled on small cylinders no larger than a walking stick. That system of storage is suited to maintain an old tradition, it saves space and makes handling convenient, but it is not very good for the paintings. They have done surprisingly well because they are seldom unrolled and because there is a kind of discipline and drill in the way they are handled, but they have suffered a great deal of damage from being rolled, particularly those which are not ink paintings and have a definite paint film that will buckle and flake under strain. In time these works on paper or thin fabric, mounted with an aqueous adhesive on more paper or fabric at the back, tend to shape themselves to the rolled form and, when they are extended, show a series of ridges spaced by the measure of the roll's circumference (Figure

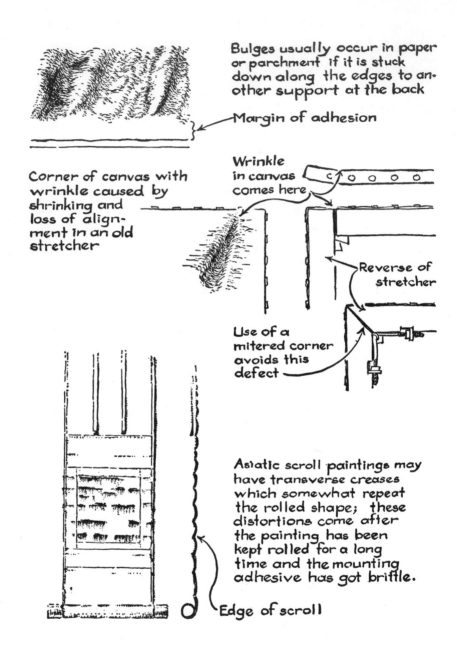

Bulges usually occur in paper or parchment if it is stuck down along the edges to another support at the back

Margin of adhesion

Corner of canvas with wrinkle caused by shrinking and loss of alignment in an old stretcher

Wrinkle in canvas comes here

Reverse of stretcher

Use of a mitered corner avoids this defect

Asiatic scroll paintings may have transverse creases which somewhat repeat the rolled shape; these distortions come after the painting has been kept rolled for a long time and the mounting adhesive has got brittle.

Edge of scroll

FIGURE 21 · DISTORTION OF THIN SUPPORTS

21). They were made that way and were intended for that kind of storage. Perhaps that is enough to excuse the practice.

Grooves and wrinkles, bulges, and other distortions of thin supports are easily seen at the face of a picture and may be disfiguring to the design (Figure 21). In paper or parchment, the most frequent cause is uneven shrinkage of the material in consequence of its being attached and held down at the edges (Plate XVIII). The practice of sticking down a drawing or print by an entire border which is pasted or glued to a mount has long since been given up as detrimental, but many works still have it. Occasionally a paper support is found pasted throughout the whole area. The mount is apt to bulge from the traction of the adhesive layer and, if air pockets form between the original support and the mount, the paper may tear. Paper or parchment in moderate size, kept in a window mat (Figure 29), needs only a small pair of hinges for attachment, and much of the work of conservation of such pictures is to free them from the strain and the other damage of unnecessary adhesives. Paintings on fabric held on a stretcher often get wrinkled and drawn. This flaw will be worse if they contain a great deal of glue in the support. During damp weather some large canvases hang limp and uneven. Small bulges start in these supports, as they start in mounted paper, where a relining adhesive has come loose and an air pocket opens between the original support and the later one put behind it.

Heavily painted pictures with complex construction, particularly those made with oil on thin supports, are not affected by darkening or stains in the fabric that carries them. Ink paintings or drawings, however, are made with the paper, silk, or parchment as an important tone in the design. Change of this tone interferes with the design. The interference is greatest when the discoloration is in particular spots or streaks, like the small, scattered, brown stains known as foxing (Figure 22 and Plate XIX). Any stains that lie in that kind of a pattern are likely to be called "foxing," and there are probably many causes for

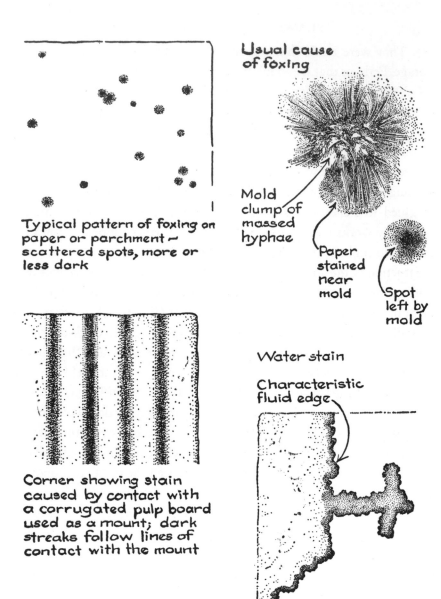

Usual cause
of foxing

Typical pattern of foxing on
paper or parchment ~
scattered spots, more or
less dark

Mold
clump of
massed
hyphae

Paper
stained
near
mold

Spot
left by
mold

Corner showing stain
caused by contact with
a corrugated pulp board
used as a mount; dark
streaks follow lines of
contact with the mount

Water stain

Characteristic
fluid edge

FIGURE 22 · DISCOLORATION OF THIN SUPPORTS

these discolorations. If they come from impurities in the paper, little can be done to prevent them, except to avoid undue dampness. This is a good measure to take in any case, for a usual kind of spotting or foxing is found to be definitely the result of the growth of mold. Possibly the mold plant, by the food it draws from the cellulose, changes it and turns it brown. It may be also that a decomposition of the mold leaves stains in the fiber. This kind of growth is much aggravated by the presence of glue sizing or a glue adhesive used in mounting, and it is almost sure to start as soon as the air around the object reaches a relative humidity of 65 percent or higher.

For drawings and prints, by far the best measures against discoloration are to prevent or to get rid of the elements that might cause it. The following conditions should be provided:

1. Clean, dry storage
2. Freedom from any adhesive at the reverse or edges
3. Freedom from contact with wood or wood-pulp pasteboard (Figure 22 and Plates XIX and XX)
4. Slight fumigation such as can be done with thymolized paper placed in the container with the pictures
5. Frequent inspection of condition

Those complex constructions—paintings on canvas that have a ground over the fabric and a surface coating over the paint and are stretched on a wooden frame for further support—can not be handled and stored as are prints and drawings. When the fabric gets weak, it may show small tears at the edges and plainly look too fragile to be hung or moved. It may not even be able to maintain its own weight on a stretcher. For centuries it has been the practice to reline such pictures, that is to attach another fabric at the back of the original one with an adhesive. Until about 1900 some kind of glue, a combination of glue with paste, some related emulsion and, rarely, a mixture of white lead and oil, were among the regular adhesives used.

They all caused much trouble and some damage. The normal changes of dampness and dryness made glue swell and shrink and the support wrinkle or bulge and then get taut again. This loosened the paint. The whole construction was apt to get very brittle and to tear easily. Mold grew in it. These defects were perhaps most noticeable in the damp climate of the Netherlands, and there experts in charge of the treatment of pictures developed a method of using wax combinations instead of the glue (Figure 23, Appendix A, 4, and Plate XXII). These adhesives were more difficult to prepare and to work, but their advantages in the conservation of fabrics and in the general stability of pictures of this type have now been established. The relining treatment is more or less standard and, briefly, takes the following procedure:

1. Application of paper to the face of the picture with a light paste adhesive (It goes without saying that the paint has been thoroughly examined and is known to be resistant to the moisture involved in this application; surface coating over the paint is sometimes left in place during this stage of the process.)
2. Removal of the old relining fabric, mechanical cleaning of the reverse of the original fabric support and extraction of any excess glue sizing which may be present (Plate XXII)
3. Attachment of relining fabric to the original fabric with a wax adhesive—a small proportion of resin is usually added to the wax —the adhesive being kept fluid by mild heat (Appendix A, 4)
4. Stretching, removal of facing, and further steps in the treatment as required

The relining process as described above somewhat darkens the fabric of the original support by the addition of the wax. No such treatment could be imagined for drawings or other pictures in which the support takes part in the design. The treatment of these, as has already been said, consists in freeing them from adhesive and from mounting materials. If they are torn, they need to be mended in order to permit

Mounting of paper or parchment with adhesive is avoided; breaks or tears are mended by rebuilding in the damaged area

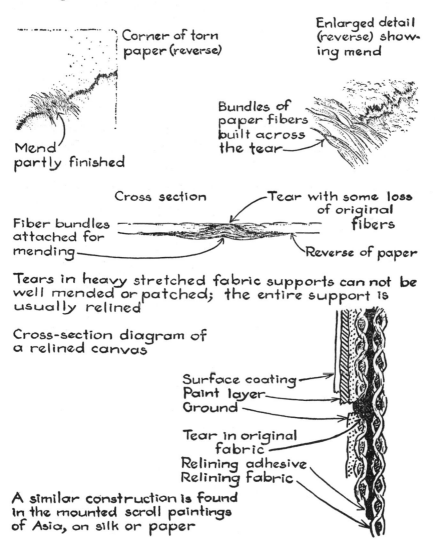

Corner of torn paper (reverse)

Enlarged detail (reverse) showing mend

Mend partly finished

Bundles of paper fibers built across the tear

Cross section

Tear with some loss of original fibers

Fiber bundles attached for mending

Reverse of paper

Tears in heavy stretched fabric supports can not be well mended or patched; the entire support is usually relined

Cross-section diagram of a relined canvas

Surface coating
Paint layer
Ground

Tear in original fabric
Relining adhesive
Relining fabric

A similar construction is found in the mounted scroll paintings of Asia, on silk or paper

FIGURE 23 · REPAIR OF THIN SUPPORTS

safe handling. The usual method is to rebuild the tear with paper fibers (Figure 23). These form a kind of mechanical bond, but the attachment is improved by a very dilute addition of starch or flour paste. Bundles of the mending fiber are laid across the tear at the reverse in such a way that the thickness of the paper is only slightly increased and such that there is no line at the edge of the mend.

In most respects, the treatment of flaws in thin supports is more satisfactory than in panels. Supports of metal in themselves give little trouble, although they have a weak bond with paint and ground, and cleavage from them is common. Stone, if broken, can be mended with an appropriate cement and the back of it reinforced. Plaster and even clay can be strengthened. These supports are few in most collections, and the wooden panel is the common problem.

The most noticeable defect in wood is its warp. With the best of intentions, a great deal of harm has been done in an attempt to flatten such panels and keep them flat (Figure 24). They can be flattened, temporarily at least. Almost without exception, they warp so that the paint lies on the outer and longer surface, the inner and shorter part of the curve coming at the back. A good share of the cause of warping is the loss of moisture and an unrestricted chance to shrink on the uncoated surface. If more moisture is put in, the panel will regain something of its flat character, but in normal housing the moisture can not be kept there. Trials have been made to keep the wood damp by putting glycerine into the back, and some improvement has been claimed as a result, but no controlled tests have been reported.

Correction of warping stands as an unsolved problem. Heavy strips or bars have been glued and screwed across the back of the panel. It does not take long to find that this is a poor system. Shrinking again where the water has gone out of the fiber, the wood is caught by this restraint and it cracks. Various means have been devised with the aim of letting the wood shrink and still stay flat. The so-called "cradle" is one of these (Figure 24). It is a kind of lattice. Pieces of wood notched

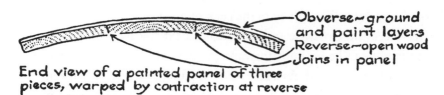

Obverse~ground
and paint layers
Reverse~open wood
Joins in panel

End view of a painted panel of three
pieces, warped by contraction at reverse

A warped panel can be flattened by dampening at the
reverse but tends to recover its curve on drying

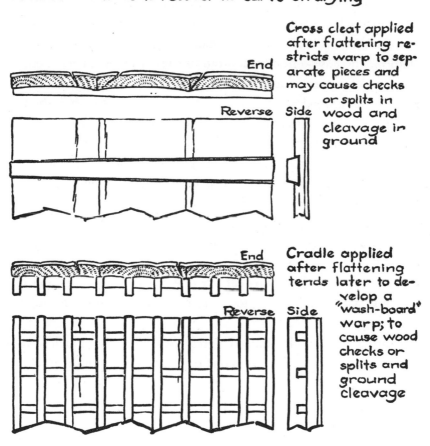

End

Reverse Side

Cross cleat applied
after flattening re-
stricts warp to sep-
arate pieces and
may cause checks
or splits in
wood and
cleavage in
ground

End

Reverse Side

Cradle applied
after flattening
tends later to de-
velop a
"wash-board"
warp; to
cause wood
checks or
splits and
ground
cleavage

FIGURE 24 · WARPING IN WOOD SUPPORTS
AND ATTEMPTS TO FLATTEN THEM

on the under side are glued to the back of a panel along the grain, and free pieces lie crosswise in the notches, next the old wood. A good argument can be brought forward in favor of this device, but it has not worked very well. As a rule, the old panel is shaved down thinner before the cradle is put on, but the stubborn habit of the warped wood can not be broken. It works toward its natural distortion. Crosspieces of the cradle get pinched and locked. A kind of wash-board warp is likely to develop. Small cracks show up, and cleavage between ground and wood seems more extensive than in panels that have not been cradled. There is no neat solution to this problem. As in most other problems of conservation, a little prevention is far ahead of any cure. If at the start a wood panel is to be used as a painting support, it should be of quartered wood so that both sides will have about the same character, and it should be given the same kind of coating on both sides. The back does not need to have a picture, but it should get the same ground, the same general type of paint layer, and a similar surface coating. That can be done only for pictures in the making. For old pictures any courses of action that are known are all more or less unsatisfactory: to leave the warped wood alone and seal the reverse as far as possible from further rapid change of moisture content; to weaken the wood slightly by cutting it along the grain lines and rebuilding, with a seal added; to transfer the ground and paint to another support.

Transfer has been dramatized a great deal. There is a touch of the sensational in taking paint from one panel and putting it on another. When the procedure was first developed, it was often used, and now, after more than a hundred years, the detriment to pictures from unwise use has become more evident. Now and again it is necessary (Appendix A, 9, and Plate XII), but no experienced operator undertakes this type of treatment unless the situation demands it. It does not involve extraordinary risks if done with knowledge and caution, but the advantages may not be worth what risk there is or the great

Complete removal of supporting material is done only when extreme risk to a painting requires it; transfer is rare with fabric supports

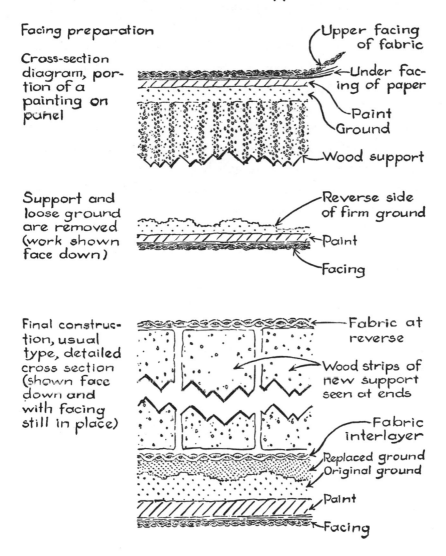

Facing preparation

Cross-section diagram, portion of a painting on panel

Upper facing of fabric

Under facing of paper

Paint

Ground

Wood support

Support and loose ground are removed (work shown face down)

Reverse side of firm ground

Paint

Facing

Final construction, usual type, detailed cross section (shown face down and with facing still in place)

Fabric at reverse

Wood strips of new support seen at ends

Fabric interlayer

Replaced ground
Original ground

Paint

Facing

FIGURE 25 · TRANSFER OF SUPPORTS

time and expense that have to be taken. The usual broad description of transfer—removal of paint from one panel to another—is misleading. It would be better to describe the process as a removal and rebuilding of a support (Figure 25). The paint and ground are given a provisional support at the front while the original panel is still in place. Then the old support can be taken off, leaving the paint and ground intact (Appendix A, 7). At the back of the ground a new support is built, and it is usually a composite construction (Appendix A, 7, and Plate XXIII). After that is complete, the provisional support at the front, a heavy facing, is taken off. In general, unless a warped panel is extreme in its curve and has begun to cause cleavage of ground or paint, it had better be left alone with firm but free support in the frame and a seal against quick passage of moisture.

Except for cracking, the other kinds of damage to wood are not serious. It does get weak and uneven in texture. Rarely this may be caused by dry rot, a kind of fungus, but the main cause of uneven weakening is the action of the larvae of beetles. In temperate climates and in buildings that have central heating and regular cleaning, the larvae of beetles—worms—are not a threat to detached panel pictures. If worms infested the panel in the past, however, they may have left the wood in a poor state. Cleavage is somewhat more apt to occur over areas that are badly tunneled by worms (Figure 19), and the wood is inconsistent and hard to seal against changes of moisture. These weak parts can be taken out and replaced with a fill of light and plastic material (Figure 26 and Appendix A, 8).

It is a natural mistake to think that a strong piece of wood is the best support for an old painting. Some experience with pictures suggests that the stronger the wood, the greater is the strain on ground and paint. The strain may be disrupting after those layers have lost their early resilience. As long as it serves to prevent mechanical damage, the weaker the panel, the better. Even though it is perforated by worm holes and softened by rot, it is heavier and tougher than most

Where a support has uneven strains because of any weakness, rebuilding can improve consistency and allow a better seal against moisture

Portion of panel at reverse shows marks of weakening by worms (beetle larvae)

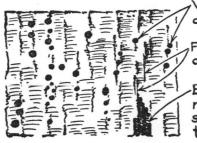

Worm holes at surface

Fine checks over tunnels

Broken wood near edge showing tunnels

Cross section of part of panel

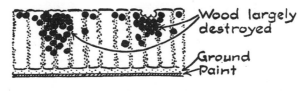

Wood largely destroyed

Ground
Paint

Reverse with weakened portions cut out

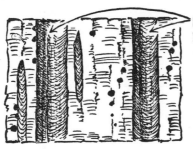

Firm wood below tunneled areas

Cross section after repair

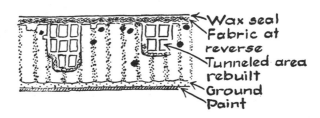

Wax seal
Fabric at reverse
Tunneled area rebuilt
Ground
Paint

FIGURE 26 · REPAIR OF PARTIAL DAMAGE IN WOOD

canvas and has no more weight to carry. All measures calculated to improve the condition of supports, particularly those which are aimed at keeping the support from undue expansion and contraction, are only partial in their results. The natural materials which respond to moisture can not be kept from that response, and in most buildings moisture changes can not be kept away from them. Improvement has come from sealing panel paintings into air-tight containers. The greatest good is complete air conditioning of storage or exhibition areas. For all purposes, a relative humidity level around 55 percent will ward off much of the damage that comes to supporting materials and, more important than that, if it is a steady level, it will ward off most of the damage to paint caused by the activity of the support under it.

6 · Housing, Handling, and Moving

MOST of the damages and defects which have been reviewed in the foregoing chapters could have been avoided. A picture that is moderately well built could be preserved for an incalculable time. Put it into an airtight container, completely clean and dust-free, completely free from shock and vibration, and hold it at a dead level of temperature fixed somewhere above freezing and below 100°F. and at a dead level of relative humidity fixed somewhere between 45 and 60 percent. (The temperature and relative humidity in this perfect housing would have to be adjusted according to the materials in the particular picture.) Let in a measured amount of diffuse white light and have the interior visible. Above all, keep every condition constant at every hour and minute of every day. Except for the unmanageable hazards of great calamities, storm and earthquake and war, this could be done. Within reasonable limits it has been done. A few museums and galleries have been able to keep the whole interior of their establishments consistently suited to the conservation of the objects in them. There is no better way to take care of pictures than to control the air conditions and maintain a stable temperature and a stable relative humidity twenty-four hours of the day and during every day of the year. But this can not be done in many collections, and to keep particular pictures hidden away in special nurseries would make them useless to men and would violate the reason for their existence.

Most pictures have to live along with people and, with them, take a few chances. Care of pictures, in the housing they will usually get, must take into account the kinds and the extent of those chances, to thwart or counter the agencies of damage and deterioration. The most destructive agency is fire. If it does not completely destroy paint, paper, wood, or fabric, it may char them until they have lost their meaning, smoke them until they are defaced, or heat them until they melt or break. Water is almost as bad. As a fluid, spilled or dropped from leaks or condensed on a surface, it can change the tone of pigments, blanch resinous coatings, dissolve mediums, and set up internal cleavage because of uneven swelling. As a vapor in the air at high concentration, it tends to soften and expand organic material, to accelerate chemical and photochemical interaction, and particularly to start mold growing. Shock, such as jolting or bumping, and vibration aggravate the loosening of paint or ground where there is partial cleavage. Excess light, especially direct sunlight or prolonged daylight, will fade certain colors and will hasten the darkening and weakening of the cellulose fiber in paper and fabric. Unbroken darkness causes discoloration of oils and augments the development of mold and fungi. Dust, besides its own discoloration, tends to hold moisture and adds to the chance for growth of mold. In addition to these there are the hazards of household accidents. Accidents are more apt to occur if pictures are moved and rehung frequently or if small ones are often handled. The risks that go with packing and shipping are not very different from those of housing except in degree. All of the chances against a picture are multiplied when the picture is transported. Irregularities of temperature and dampness are practically unavoidable, and so are extensive shock and vibration.

A great deal can be done to protect a picture by housing it in a suitable frame. Observations over a period of about thirty years have given good reason to believe that paintings set into a frame which is, in effect, an airtight box have held their condition far better than similar works exposed to the air. Such a frame need not be extremely heavy or cumbersome. It needs to have the glass sealed, to have the face of the picture some distance behind that, and to have a tight backing (Figure 27). This framing keeps out dirt, it protects the pic-

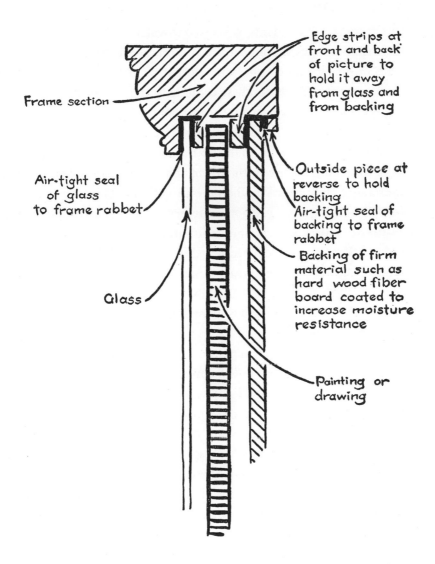

Edge strips at front and back of picture to hold it away from glass and from backing

Frame section

Air-tight seal of glass to frame rabbet

Outside piece at reverse to hold backing

Air-tight seal of backing to frame rabbet

Backing of firm material such as hard wood fiber board coated to increase moisture resistance

Glass

Painting or drawing

FIGURE 27 · PICTURE SEALED IN A FRAME
CROSS-SECTION DIAGRAM

ture from minor accidents, it keeps out water, and it reduces extreme and rapid changes of temperature and relative humidity. Small variations in the air outside the frame do not penetrate it. Even the long, slow changes in the air as these come with the seasons and with heating systems can be modified if the interior of the frame case is made to hold a fair amount of absorbent material such as wood or fabric. It must be more absorbent than the materials of the picture and, if it is, it takes up moisture in the air of the closed space when moisture is excessive and releases it when the air gets dry. This type of framing for large pictures has had some further advance—particularly at the National Gallery of Scotland, Edinburgh—through a device which holds different salts calculated to aid in keeping an equilibrium in the relative humidity inside the case (Plate XXIV). A pair of salts, among those available, is the hepta- and hexahydrates of zinc sulphate. These are at equilibrium in an atmosphere of 55 percent relative humidity at a temperature of 60° F.

Relative humidity, to review the matter, is the proportion of moisture in the air in relation to the temperature. Dampness is somewhat dependent on temperature. Figures for relative humidity are given in percent—the percent of moisture in the air of a particular locality as a proportion of the total amount of moisture which the air at that temperature might contain. Atmospheric pressure has some influence but not enough to be considered here. If, for example, at 70° F. the air holds four grains per cubic foot of moisture, the relative humidity is 50 percent. At that temperature the air could hold twice that amount of moisture. Absolute humidity, as distinct from relative, is the amount of moisture measured as water in the air of a particular locality. The absolute humidity is not very important in the care of pictures or other objects of art. Dampness, as we commonly experience it, is a matter of relative humidity, the amount of moisture in the surrounding air in relation to the amount that the air at that temperature might hold. This varies directly with temperature. At 40° F. the air will hold 2.9 grains of water vapor in each cubic foot; at 70° it will hold 8 grains; at 100° it will hold 19.8. As the schoolboy knows, that is the cause of rain; warm air saturated with water vapor, on being cooled, precipitates the water that it can not longer hold in a vapor form.

The various materials in pictures respond unevenly to moisture; this uneven response is the cause of strain between support and ground and is the cause of most of the cleavage, flaking, and peeling of paint. A high relative humidity, particularly for panel pictures, would help relieve such strain if that humidity could be kept constant. It would, however, increase the chance for the growth of mold. A good level, safe from risk of mold growth but high enough to keep wood panels, parchment, and sized canvas from getting too dry, is 55 percent relative humidity. In a temperate climate the range in houses that are not air-conditioned is extreme. Central heating during cold weather brings down relative humidity often to a level between 10 and 20 percent. During the damp summer months it will rise to 90 percent.

In collections where some of the pictures are kept stored, the housing can be managed with occasional change of objects and avoidance of the worst extremes of dampness and dryness. A tight room with moderate light, suitable for use as a storage area, can often be found in an upper floor space of a house and given appropriate racking and shelving (Figure 28). An upper floor location can be allowed to stay hot in the summer, and that will help to keep the relative humidity down. In the winter it can be kept cool, and that will avoid a dangerous drop in relative humidity. It is important that such a room be tight, closed, and kept closed. Rapid changes in the conditions of the air out of doors are not apt to occur in a closed space. Such a room should be kept in order, clear and easy of access, and clean. Things should be clean and dust-free when they go into it (Figure 30). Grime that settles on pictures is disfiguring and possibly damaging, and it is very hard to get off. Without much doubt, efforts to remove so-called

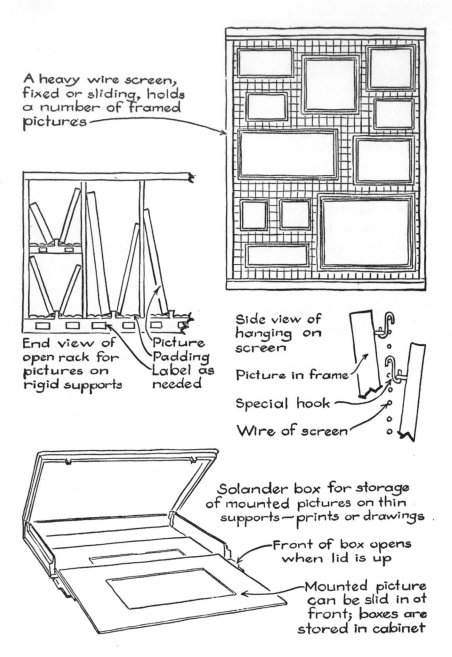

A heavy wire screen, fixed or sliding, holds a number of framed pictures

End view of open rack for pictures on rigid supports

Picture Padding Label as needed

Side view of hanging on screen

Picture in frame

Special hook

Wire of screen

Solander box for storage of mounted pictures on thin supports — prints or drawings

Front of box opens when lid is up

Mounted picture can be slid in at front; boxes are stored in cabinet

FIGURE 28 · STORAGE

"plain dirt" have done more injury to the paint of pictures than have the procedures of varnish removal. Dirt is worst on paper such as prints, drawings, and water colors and on the scroll pictures of Asia. The old and the sound practice is to keep these in tight boxes (Figure 28).

If a picture on a thin support is to be either framed for hanging or boxed for storage, it needs a suitable mount. It can not be handled safely without that auxiliary support. Throughout the West a somewhat standard system is now adopted for such mounting. Paper boards are used, and the first requirement is that these shall be of pure rag fiber. Pulp boards have caused irreparable damage when left in contact with good paper. On the mounting board the original thin support is fastened at the back by small tabs or hinges attached with paste. A window mat, a cut-out border, fits over the mount leaving the picture free (Fig. 29). Usually a thin slip sheet is laid, for protection, over the picture and under the window mat.

In a closed storage room the risk of mold growth or of the inroads of bugs and worms can be largely averted. Cleanliness helps to keep them away, and the air can be poisoned against them. Many different fumigants for that purpose have been tried, and most of them do some good. Most volatile substances seem to bother fungi and insects. Camphor, naphthalene, and paradichlorobenzene are probably the most common fumigants in the houses of Europe and the Western Hemisphere. In the Far East, aromatic woods such as sandalwood are used and, though probably less effective, are more pleasant to have around. Perhaps the most effective against both mold and insects is paradichlorobenzene. In a tight storage room the crystals of this toxic material should be placed at a high level, for the vapor is heavier than air. Another material, toxic particularly to insects, is carbon tetrachloride, familiar as a cleaner for spots on clothing. This fluid could be vaporized from a container with a wick or sponge. The vapor is heavier than

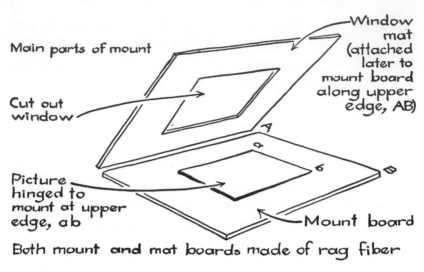

Main parts of mount

Cut out window

Window mat (attached later to mount board along upper edge, AB)

A

a

b

B

Picture hinged to mount at upper edge, ab

Mount board

Both mount and mat boards made of rag fiber

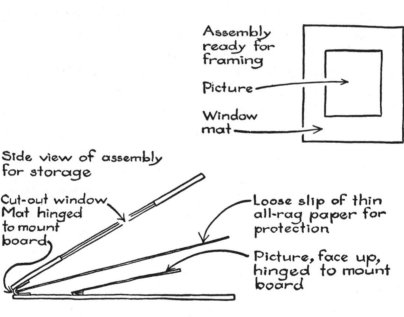

Assembly ready for framing

Picture

Window mat

Side view of assembly for storage

Cut-out window. Mat hinged to mount board

Loose slip of thin all-rag paper for protection

Picture, face up, hinged to mount board

FIGURE 29 · MOUNTING THIN SUPPORTS
AS USUALLY DONE FOR PRINTS
AND DRAWINGS

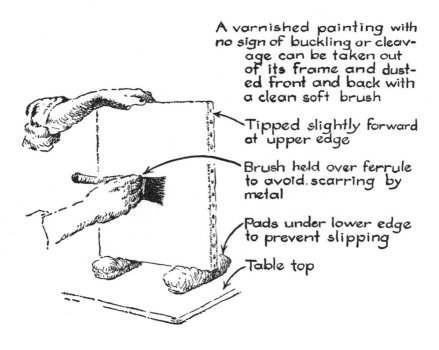

A varnished painting with no sign of buckling or cleavage can be taken out of its frame and dusted front and back with a clean soft brush

Tipped slightly forward at upper edge

Brush held over ferrule to avoid scarring by metal

Pads under lower edge to prevent slipping

Table top

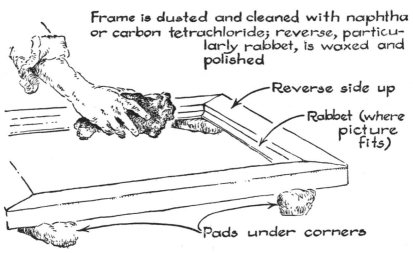

Frame is dusted and cleaned with naphtha or carbon tetrachloride; reverse, particularly rabbet, is waxed and polished

Reverse side up

Rabbet (where picture fits)

Pads under corners

FIGURE 30 · DUSTING

air. It might be able to serve a double duty for it is also a fire extinguisher.

The means provided for putting out house fires are an important factor in the care of pictures. The most damaging of common fire extinguishers is the soda-acid type. This can usually be recognized by its descriptive name on the metal container or by the instructions for using it. The soda-acid extinguisher has to be inverted as a rule; turning it upside down dumps a quantity of acid into a bed of soda and releases a stream of water containing carbon dioxide. This in itself would do no more harm than water alone, but there is liable to be an excess of acid carried also by the water of solution. The best type of fire extinguisher is pure carbon dioxide gas. In museum storage areas this is ready to be thrown into the rooms through installed pipe conduits which carry the gas from cylinders to ceiling vents. From these it is released either by throwing a switch or, in most cases, by a special thermostatic control. Smaller units for hand operation are available. Preparations have been made of sodium bicarbonate as a fire extinguisher. They are moderately effective if used quickly on small fires and do not damage pictures. The soda is thrown on the flame as a powder and tends to smother combustion and to release carbon dioxide. Dry, clean sand will do little harm and can quickly smother small flames. Water can do a great deal of harm, but injury from water is far less serious than injury from fire. The important thing is to put the fire out.

A few suggestions are given in Figures 31 to 33 concerning the handling, hanging, and packing of pictures. Specific instructions on these matters are, in reality, far less useful than is a sensible understanding of the needs of each particular object. Most damage during the handling or transport of pictures comes from failure to consider their actual weakness and the probable risks they will run, and from failure to provide simple means to guard against such risks. Think of a picture in all cases as an object that is fragile, that could be damaged

Removal from wall

Steadied at the top

Supported at the bottom

Carrying

Only small pictures can be safely carried by one person

Large works need two carriers

Face of picture is held toward carriers for better protection

End view of rolling truck used to carry large pictures

FIGURE 31 · HANDLING

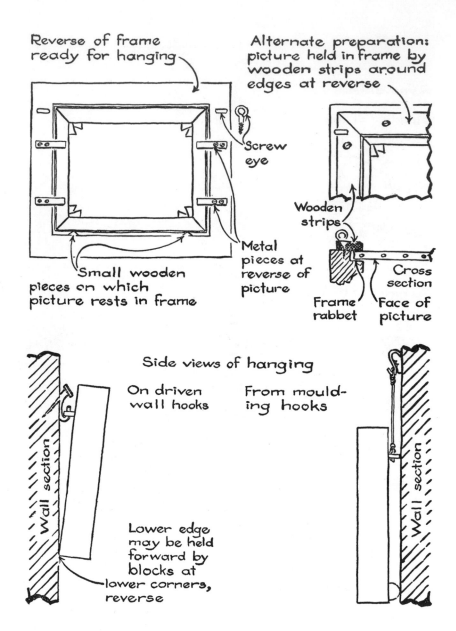

Reverse of frame ready for hanging

Alternate preparation: picture held in frame by wooden strips around edges at reverse

Screw eye

Small wooden pieces on which picture rests in frame

Metal pieces at reverse of picture

Wooden strips

Cross section

Frame rabbet

Face of picture

Side views of hanging

On driven wall hooks

From mould-ing hooks

Wall section

Lower edge may be held forward by blocks at lower corners, reverse

Wall section

FIGURE 32 · HANGING FRAMED PICTURES

by a thumb nail or a sleeve button. Before picking up a framed picture, look carefully to see what it is, how it is fixed in the frame, and where you can safely take hold of it. If it is a work on paper or on silk, consider that it may be torn by the slightest pull or strain, that oil in the skin of the human hand can leave a mark on it, and that it has to be put on a surface which is smooth and dry and completely clean. If the object is to be carried (Figure 31), know how it can be fully supported and steadied, make certain that the way to be taken is clear and lighted, and that the place where it is to be put is ready for it. If it is to be hung (Figure 32), see to it that the hardware used, the hooks, eyes, and wires, are strong, well placed, and well fitted together.

If the picture is to be packed, figure on how it is to be loaded and handled and unpacked, what risks may lie ahead of dampness, vibration, and dust. Packing in most cases is a job for experts, but they may not always be at hand when they are needed. If you have to prepare a picture for shipment, think first of possible damage and then of ways to avoid it. Specific rules are poor in this as in most procedures, but a few general principles are worth keeping in mind:

1. The whole outer packing should be tight against dust and weather.
2. The outer packing should cushion the picture in all directions.
3. An inner package should protect the picture from any possible rubbing, puncture, bending, or soiling.
4. There should be no loose parts in the assembly of picture and frame.
5. Tacks or nails should be avoided during the packing. The vibration from hammering may be as damaging as that from transport; a wooden box can be nailed together before hand but, after the picture is packed in it, the top should be fastened with screws. These also make unpacking much safer.
6. Packing material should be resilient, with enough spring to keep

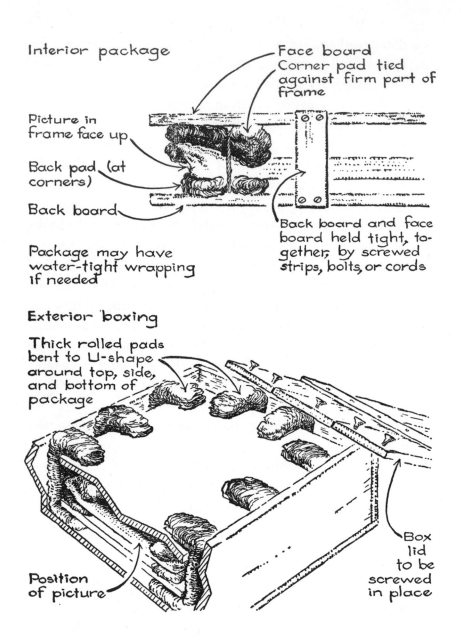

Interior package

Face board
Corner pad tied
against firm part of
frame

Picture in
frame face up

Back pad (at
corners)

Back board

Back board and face
board held tight, to-
gether, by screwed
strips, bolts, or cords

Package may have
water-tight wrapping
if needed

Exterior boxing

Thick rolled pads
bent to U-shape
around top, side,
and bottom of
package

Position
of picture

Box
lid
to be
screwed
in place

FIGURE 33 · A PACKING FOR FRAMED PICTURES

from wadding. Such materials are far more effective in rolls or pads than as loose fiber. Excelsior or wood wool, dried Spanish moss, shredded paper, crumpled tissue paper, felt, hair, and sponge rubber have all been used effectively as packing materials.

All of these precautions seem fastidious against the background of the past. If the stories of many old pictures could be read in their entirety, they would tell of hardships—of being carried through dusty and sun-beaten streets in processions, of the smoke of candles and the varnish pot of the houseman, of hauls through bad weather and with scant cover, of storage in moldy cellars, and of jolts at the loading dock. By comparison, expert handling and air conditioning may seem fussy and foolish. But the pictures themselves tell a story of weakness. The hard life has not made them stronger, and, if they are to be kept, certain rational precautions are needed in handling them. These are fairly simple, and, at the cost of some repetition, they can be reviewed.

1. Consider carefully the needs of each particular picture, and bring those needs to the attention of any persons who may have to handle it.
2. Inspect pictures frequently whether they are in living rooms, exhibition galleries, or storage.
3. Make certain that each picture is securely placed and, as far as possible, free from the hazards of minor accidents.
4. Look into the condition of fire risks and of fire-fighting equipment.
5. Consult an expert when there is any question of condition or procedure.
6. Keep a record of condition with notes on defects and irregularities and on any changes or repairs.

The last point is more important than it may appear. Deterioration of pictures is a matter of very slow progress. The eye becomes accustomed to each imperceptible stage of this progress, and the long change is never seen. A few notes, dated and with any questions or observations, may serve to indicate the speed at which damage is progressing. They will show also the trials and the errors that have been made in efforts to save and maintain a thing that, in the last count, must be rated as impermanent.

Appendix A · Record Abstracts of Repair Treatment

THE FOLLOWING are brief summaries of laboratory notes on a few works that have been treated for purposes of repair. These are very brief abstracts. The procedures they record are not by any means the only ones which might have been used. They are merely examples of what was done in certain cases over a period of fifteen years. There are few fixed, standard procedures, none that does not have to be modified to suit the needs of each particular work. These examples will review some of the problems of repair and some of the efforts to solve them. A few of the examples have been previously published in greater detail. Particularly to be acknowledged is the privilege of using, in Example 11, information from "A Method of Cleaning Prints," by Sheldon Keck in *Technical Studies in the Field of the Fine Arts,* Volume V (1936), pages 117–26.

1. *Removal of a Soft Resin Coating from a Paint Containing Soft Resin— Two Examples*

a. The painting was French, made in the third quarter of the nineteenth century. The surface coating was heavy, moderately discolored, and extremely brittle. The last defect had caused a crazing with a resulting yellowish tone which changed all of the paint color and particularly the darks. These had lost definition and depth of value. To some extent, varnish was responsible also for a general buckling of the paint along crackle lines. The canvas support had sagged and was wrinkled at the corners. The size of the painting was 1.000 × 0.815 meter.

A facing of mulberry paper was attached with rice paste over the surface coating, and the light linen support was relined with a wax adhesive (beeswax with 20 percent of dammar resin and gum elemi) and stretched. This was done to give adequate support and to correct the buckling of ground and paint. The facing was removed.

Usual solvents such as the alcohols and ketones, which are not active on a hardened layer of oil paint, softened the paint of this picture in microscopic trials, and it was evident that this paint had been mixed with a large component of a soft resin. The difference of solubility, therefore, of the paint proper and the surface coating was relative to the speed of action of the solvent and the time during which the solvent was allowed to act.

Following a number of experimental trials, the solvent mixture adopted was petroleum naphtha, 2 parts, carbon tetrachloride, 2 parts, xylene, 1 part, and diacetone alcohol, 1 part. This was applied with a small pointed sable brush in a field that was observed with 5X magnification. The means of application prevented any rubbing of the paint. As soon as the surface film had gone into solution, it was taken up on an absorbent cotton pad covered with gauze and slightly dampened with petroleum naphtha. Naphtha had no solvent action on either varnish or paint.

b. An American painting, dated 1897, was thinly executed in what appeared to be an oil medium but was found to have a solubility which showed that a large content of soft resin had been used with the oil. The support, 0.430 × 0.360 meter, was a prepared linen canvas with a thin ground of white. There was no buckling or other structural defect, but the work was disfigured by a heavy surface coating of soft resin which had turned brown and obliterated fine relations of color and value.

Clearing of this surface coating was done by solution in xylene. The solvent was put on to a small area at a time, about 5 centimeters across, being applied with a soft brush. It was kept in a thick, fluid condition for about ten minutes, and in this time the surface film was swollen to a gelled state. The paint beneath it was not affected.

A small swab of absorbent cotton, dampened with xylene, took up the remaining solvent on the area treated and rolled off the gelled surface film. The area was then brushed freely with turpentine to take up any remaining particles of the surface coating, and the turpentine was lifted on absorbent cotton.

Areas treated in immediate sequence were not adjacent to each other, and any solvent remaining had time to dry thoroughly before the edge of a treated area was in contact with a later application. So far as possible, the shapes of the areas treated were kept to individual parts of the pattern of representation in order to avoid any chance of disfigurement from remaining lines or streaks of the darkened surface coating.

2. *Clearing of Surface Coating and Overpainting from an Italian Panel Picture*

The painting was a part of a predella made about 1300; the size, 0.436 × 0.438 meter. The panel was in good condition, a thick piece of poplar with no sign of previous treatment except that of removal from the large altarpiece of which it had formerly been a small part. There was no evidence of cleavage and practically no distortion of the support. The surface was heavily coated with stained varnish and underneath that was an extensive overpainting done evidently with the intention of having it look like the workmanship of the fourteenth century (Plate XIII). The medium seemed to be largely resinous.

Preliminary examination had established the solubility of surface coating and overpaint and had indicated that the areas of loss in the original paint were much smaller than the extent of later work would normally indicate. Removal of these later coatings was carried out by the usual process of dissolving them in suitable solvents. A mixture of acetone, 2 parts, with diacetone alcohol, 1 part, brought these coating materials into solution, acting very slowly but effectively on the overpaint.

When the readily soluble stain and later paint had been taken off, splatters of a brown material, like the oil stains used for furniture, were found in parts of the gold ground. In behavior this seemed to be an oil film, and its obvious irregular shape showed that it had been spilled or splashed on to the surface by accident. Removal of these stains was possible with an instrument after the film material had been softened by an application of the following mixture: triethanolamine, 5 parts, dibutyl phthalate, 5 parts, cellosolve, 10 parts, ammonium hydroxide, 10 parts, acetone, 10 parts, morpholine, 10 parts.

Losses in the paint were compensated with tempera, followed by slight final corrections in an oil medium. The surface coating was a thin film of polymerized vinyl acetate and, after this had dried for a few months, hard wax was put over it and polished.

3. *Removal of Grime from the Surface of an Ancient Wax Painting*

The fragment of a mummy painting on thin wood and executed in a wax medium had been brought to the United States in about 1900 (Plate IV). The broken support was 0.325 × 0.154 meter and about 1 millimeter thick. The treatment was carried out in 1930. There had developed a good deal of cleavage and buckling between the wax paint and the wood. Irregular streaks of grime acquired during burial had never been removed. The painting was considered to have been done during the first or second century A.D.

To strengthen the support, the thin ground was backed up with quartered walnut, an application feasible in a work of this scale. Buckling was treated with a 5 percent solution of beeswax and carbon tetrachloride flowed on to the loosened areas with a long-haired sable brush. Beeswax was carried under the flakes, and the solvent slightly softened the original paint so that it could be pressed into place.

Surface grime was a tenacious deposit of brownish clay. It was found that this could be loosened if brushed with a small, soft sable carrying a dilute solution of beeswax in carbon tetrachloride. The wax component kept down the rate of evaporation and allowed the solvent to act slowly. Probably over a period of hours this mixture would have softened the original paint. Used in small areas, however, and for a few minutes at a time, it left the paint entirely hard.

4. Relining and Clearing of Discolored Varnish from an Oil Painting on Canvas

The painting was an Italian work of the eighteenth century; the size, 1.445×1.118 meter. It had been relined at least once before with glue or glue mixture as the adhesive. The general condition was normal to this type of work and moderately good as to state of preservation. The entire construction, however, was extremely brittle and subject to risk in usual conditions of exhibition and storage. There was a heavy and complex coating of varnish, evidently applied after a partial removal of an old varnish layer. This appeared as a brown residue in the grooves of paint. There were a few small tears.

To permit secure attachment of a facing, most of the discolored resinous coating was removed at the start of treatment (Plate III). The solvent mixture used was acetone, 2 parts, diacetone alcohol, 1 part. This softened the varnish but not the occasional overpaint that had been used to cover blemishes. For this overpaint a mixture of acetone, diacetone alcohol, and a small addition of ammonium hydroxide was used as a solvent. After the extraneous surface coatings had been cleared, the painting was faced with two layers of mulberry paper attached with a rice flour paste.

Stretcher and relining fabric were removed from the reverse, and the former glue adhesive was taken off by scraping (as in Plate XXII). The support was treated with thymol, 5 percent in ethyl alcohol, as a fungicide. Relining canvas was applied with a wax-resin adhesive and was stretched. Inpainting of conspicuous losses was carried out with tempera colors after the facing had been removed. The surface film applied was polyvinyl acetate, 10 percent in ethyl alcohol, followed, after thorough drying, by a thin film of hard wax.

5. *Reattachment of Paint and Ground*

A panel painting, 1.024 × 1.148 meter in size, an Umbrian work of the fifteenth century, came to an American collection in 1900. Before that time it had been largely in one church near Assisi. After about a year in the United States it was reported to have suffered greatly from the American climate. There was no record of any work having been done on it, however, until 1926. Either then or three years later—an unspecified amount of work is recorded as having been done in both those years—the painting was removed from its original panel and transferred to a firm new support of mahogany with a cradle of the same wood.

The construction after this, complicated by the transfer, included both original and later grounds, the latter in a heavy layer. Both grounds were essentially the same, a white inert material with a gelatin or skin glue as binding medium. A layer of fabric had been put between them during the transfer process. There was little gold leaf in the work, and the paint in a microscopically thin film was laid directly on the original ground or gesso.

In condition the paint had suffered some loss from flaking and extensive loss from abrasion. Later paint covered the losses and also areas of original paint. Old and irregular residues of a varnish-like layer lodged in the paint depressions. A stained and pigmented varnish had been put on at a fairly recent time. The conspicuous defect, however, was cleavage and buckling in the upper part of the original ground layer. Examination showed that the original ground had lost most of its cohesiveness and was a mealy, powdery mass from which the paint had broken loose.

The record of condition prior to 1926 does not indicate what the defect was, but it probably was cleavage. By 1936, seven years after the second treatment, the picture had reached a very fragile state. The paint in many

areas was curled into thin flakes that were too brittle to stand normal conditions of hanging. It was decided that, although the action of the mahogany
panel was partly responsible for the cleavage, it would be unwise at that
time to attempt another transfer.

The buckled paint was treated first with solvent, dropped on. This softened the surface coating and made it tacky enough to hold small pieces of
mulberry paper as facing. The cleavage pockets were later infused with a
solution of gelatin, and this application was repeated. Gelatin solution was
good for a partial reattachment, but the granular state of the ground evidently caused so much absorption of this adhesive that reattachment by
infusion was not dependable. With a facing of thin mulberry paper attached with polyvinyl acetate, hinged flakes of the paint were lifted and
reattached by a brushed application of the gelatin.

The varnish and overpaint were removed with solvents. Compensation
of losses was carried out where necessary, and a surface film of thin polyvinyl acetate was applied, followed, after an interval of months, with a
coating of wax.

After another period, this time of nine years, some buckling was evident. It was in a small and restricted area and was treated by infusion with
gelatin solution followed, after drying, by wax containing a small proportion of gum elemi. Reattachment seemed satisfactory, but it was evident
that the work contained a large amount of infirm ground and that the
action of a heavy and strong support would cause periodic buckling as the
wood was affected by changing amounts of dampness in the air.

6. Reattachment of Paint to Stone

Stone supports for pictures are rare but have been used at different
periods in the history of art. This picture was Italian, seventeenth century.
The stone was dark gray, resembling slate, and had been polished before
the paint was applied. The size was 0.310 × 0.225 meter, the thickness 15.8
millimeters. The paint was in an oil medium. At different times in the past
it had been varnished. A series of coatings of soft resin had become crazed
and darkened and they disturbed considerably the tone relations.

It was more serious that the surface coatings had stuck to the paint better
than the paint, in turn, had stuck to the stone. With the shrinkage of these
heavy resinous coatings, the paint had curled up into thin and brittle flakes
(Plate XVI). The picture had a record of having been taken repeatedly

for repair, and it was evident that repair had consisted largely in adding another layer of varnish. This had had the temporary effect of softening the coatings already in place; then of making the cleavage worse when the last one began to shrink in its turn. The cleavage finally became so bad that no further application of varnish was possible. It had never been advisable. On more than half of the surface the paint was loose from the support. A strong stream of air would have dislodged much of it.

To correct this condition, the painting was put into an air-tight chamber with the mixed vapors of acetone, ethyl alcohol, and diacetone alcohol. It stayed there for fifty minutes. By the end of that time the surface appearance showed that the resinous coatings had softened. The painting was taken out of the air-tight chamber, and strips of unsized mulberry paper were put on it in a way not to disarrange any of the loose paint. The paper stuck to the softened resin, and the attachment of the paper was improved by further exposure to solvent vapor. The scales of paint were somewhat flattened after this. The resin was allowed to dry for a few days. The whole construction was then warmed with bulb heat lamps to a temperature of about 55°C. The surface was flooded with a mixture of beeswax, 80 percent, and gum elemi, 20 percent, and this was kept fluid on the surface with a warm tacking iron until maximum penetration into the cleavage pockets had been effected.

Excess wax at the surface was removed with toluene, and the resin-saturated paper was taken off in the same process. The paint was again treated with the wax–gum elemi mixture. Final removal of this was done with petroleum naphtha. The surface coating applied to the clean paint was a very thin layer of polymerized vinyl acetate, followed by hard wax.

7. Reconstruction of a Panel Painting

An Italian fifteenth-century representation of a pope, part of a large altarpiece, had developed an extensive cleavage between ground and support. It was rectangular in shape, a thick piece of wood, 1.578 × 0.578 meter. The construction in ground and paint was normal: a thick gesso ground with paint in tempera and with some additions in oil. The condition of the paint was not good. Much of it had been thinned by abrasion, and there was a general stain combined with a residue of old varnish and some amount of overpainting.

A report had been made in 1914 to the effect that the support was "very rotten poplar." In 1928 an effort had been made to improve the condition of the support by applying a cradle. This had probably done more harm than good. Ten years later treatment was necessary to reattach the large cleavage pockets in the ground.

Surface coatings of soft resin were cleared from the paint by a solvent mixture of diacetone alcohol and acetone. Mulberry paper was attached securely with polyvinyl acetate as an adhesive. Over a second layer of this, heavier papers were attached with paste and, over all, linen was attached with glue.

At the reverse of the panel the badly worm-eaten wood was taken out (Plate XVII). Most of the longitudinal strips were left, but these were thinned to a narrower measure. In places the weakened wood had to be removed down to the reverse of the ground. For the most part, a few millimeters of it remained.

The support was rebuilt with a mixture of wax and dammar resin as an adhesive for strips of linen gauze and as the medium for a plastic filler containing jute fiber, pulverized cork, and kaolin. These materials were put in warm, just over the melting point of the wax-resin mixture. In the larger openings, strips of balsa wood were set into the plastic mixture. The fills were leveled at the reverse surface and a layer of linen was put over. Cross members of the cradle were replaced for rigidity and support of the panel's weight.

The facing was removed, residues of former varnish and overpaint were cleared away, and losses were inpainted where necessary. Application of a surface coating completed the work.

8. *Reconstruction of a Panel Support*

The painting was Flemish, of the early sixteenth century; the size, 0.965 × 0.678 meter. At some time in the past, estimated to be around the middle of the nineteenth century, this work, originally on a panel, had been transferred to two layers of linen fabric. The adhesive of the transfer was glue or a similar aqueous material. Although the paint still had the detailed conformation and the cracks and losses of a coating over wood, the support had taken on the sagged distortion often seen in a fabric. There was extensive cleavage, particularly between paint and ground. The construction was brittle and weak, and there was a certain contradiction between its appearance in detail and its appearance as a whole. Under the circumstances, the only prospect of making the work solid was to carry out another transfer. Since this was necessary, it was decided to return to a panel as the support.

Continuous wood puts such a strain on ground and paint that it is rarely used except in pictures of small size. The type of construction chosen in this instance was one that often has been used. After appropriate treatment of the surface, which included removal of the discolored surface coatings (as in Plate II) and application of a heavy facing, the fabrics were removed at the reverse. It was found that below the thick layer of glue adhesive was a layer of white paint, white lead in oil. This also had to be taken off because the cleavage lay beyond it and could not be mended while this film blocked penetration of an adhesive. Removal was slow, being done with a fine rotary burr on a small electric tool.

When the reverse of the original ground had been smoothed and any evident cleavage reattached, a secondary ground was made with plaster of Paris and size, in which were strips of knotted silk bolting cloth. The whole of this secondary ground was less than ¼ millimeter thick. It provided a continuous, homogeneous, thin support which was impervious to heat. Over it went a layer of linen attached with a wax-resin adhesive applied in a melted state at about 65°C. The panel built behind this was of redwood strips, 1 inch in section (as in Plate XXIII). These were set in a plastic mixture bound by the same wax-resin adhesive and containing chalk, China clay, and fine hardwood sawdust as inert filling materials. Small cross pieces also of redwood were cemented into grooves at the back, and the whole was covered with a layer of linen.

The procedure that followed was removal of facing, clearing away of grime at the paint surface, inpainting of the few losses, and surface coating.

9. *Assembly and Transfer of Fragments of a Wall Painting from Central China*

The available pieces of this painted wall, done in the sixteenth century, were thirty in number. All were of irregular size and shape, the largest approximately one meter by three-fourths. The construction was: (1) the wall plaster consisting of dry clay or loess, with varied fibrous ingredients; (2) over the smooth clay a wash coating of white, a priming layer; (3) color layers applied thinly in a glue or similar aqueous binding medium. The condition of the fragments at the start of the work was poor. All had breaks and large pits, flaking of ground and paint, and showed marked wear or abrasion (Plate XII). The surface had an irregular but general accretion of clay and was subject to damage from handling because of the chalky condition of all components in the construction of the wall and the painting on it.

The purpose of treatment was to bring the fragments together again in a correct and coherent composition and in a state suitable for normal housing and exhibition. Areas of scaling paint were flooded with a 5 percent solution of polyvinyl acetate in a combination of solvents, largely coal-tar hydrocarbons. After the loose flakes had been secured by this means, the surface of each fragment was brush-flooded with a series of coatings of polyvinyl acetate, also in a 5 percent solution, and application continued during an hour to insure maximum penetration.

When the impregnating material had become thoroughly hardened, pits and crevices were leveled with a putty of clay and water. This was allowed to dry, and the surface was given a slow brush-flooding of polyvinyl acetate, a 20 percent solution, followed by a brushing with pure solvent, diacetone alcohol, the surface being kept wet for about two and a half hours. A similar coating was repeated on three successive days with drying between times. When the polyvinyl acetate was thoroughly hard and was a thick-standing film, it was abraded with powdered pumice to make a good tooth for the facing. Two sheets in thickness of mulberry paper were applied with a rice flour paste. This was left to dry, and washed muslin in two layers was attached to the paper with glue containing enough hygroscopic material to remain flexible and readily soluble in water.

After drying, the work was put face down, and the clay was removed from the back until the level of the penetration at the front had been reached or until the white ground had been reached. Exposed ground was strengthened from the back. Irregularities were filled with clay bound by polyvinyl acetate, and the reverse was smoothed. The fragment was attached at the reverse to a piece of unbleached linen, again with polyvinyl acetate as the adhesive.

The facing could then be removed and each fragment handled as a thin piece. The edges were trimmed and the pieces assembled on a firm, wood-fiber composition board. When the position of each was established, it was attached to the board with polyvinyl acetate. Lacunae or gaps between the fragments were filled with a putty of clay, and excess film was cleared from the paint surface until its normal mat character had been recovered. This was done by solution, largely with toluene.

10. *Mounting of a Creased and Wrinkled Page of an Illuminated Manuscript*

The work was on vellum or parchment and was done with ink and with color. The origin was French, fourteenth century. The size, including the border, was 0.500 × 0.732 meter, a large page. The cause of the main defect had been a folding of the page at some previous time. No record existed of any treatment prior to 1938. Examination determined that, in spite of creases, wrinkles, and losses (Plate XVIII), the vellum was moderately flexible. There were stains and a general discoloration normal to its age. Evident attempts had been made to mend damaged areas with paper and glue.

Glue remaining at the reverse was removed by dampening with water and alcohol. (Alcohol was used to reduce the possible solvent action of water on ink and its swelling action on the vellum.) The work was disinfected with thymol in an airtight chamber. It was put face down on glass and slightly dampened. Another sheet of heavy glass was put over it and weighted. After three hours the distortions had been reduced only to a slight degree. The slight dampening and pressure between heavy glass slabs were repeated but did not satisfactorily correct the distortion. To minimize this the vellum was mounted and framed between two pieces of regular glass.

11. *Bleaching of Stain in an Etching, American, Eighteenth Century*

The main cause of stain was fluid from a fire extinguisher. Examination showed that the paper was of linen and cotton fiber, slightly sized, and that the ink was carbon in oil (the usual ink for printing). Both paper and ink could be treated by water immersion if normal precautions were taken. The plate size was 0.325 × 0.215 meter.

The paper had to be detached from a mount of ordinary wood-pulp cardboard. This was done in a water bath at room temperature. Three baths were used to effect bleaching. The first was composed of water, 2,700 milliliters, with a 5 percent solution of sodium hypochlorite, 150 milliliters, and concentrated hydrochloric acid, 15 milliliters. (The bath, when ready, should not change the color of litmus paper; it is practically neutral and so compounded as to release free chlorine.) A second bath was a very dilute hydrochloric acid, 0.5 milliliters of the concentrated acid in 2,700 milliliters of water. The third bath had 2 milliliters of concentrated ammonium hydroxide in 9,000 milliliters of water. (This should give an alkaline response with litmus paper to make certain that it can neutralize any remaining acid.)

The paper was left in the first or bleaching solution a short time—the number of seconds or minutes is that needed almost to remove the stains. It was then put in the bath of weak acid. When the bleaching was completed, the print was transferred to the weak ammonia solution and left about ten minutes. After that it was thoroughly rinsed in clear water. (The technique of handling paper in a bath has to be varied for different conditions. Usually the sheet is carried on plate glass. After it is thoroughly washed, the sheet is dried under observation and, in regular practice, with slight pressure to prevent distortion.)

12. *Bleaching of Wood Stain in Paper*

Stain, accompanied by some foxing, had developed in a print of about 1800, size 0.150 × 0.200 meter. The paper had been framed with a thin board pressed directly on the back of it, and discoloration from the wood had permeated the paper, giving it the pattern of the wood grain (Plate XIX).

The paper was submerged in a water bath, and discolored areas were lightly brushed with a sable. This somewhat reduced the stain by solution but did not entirely remove it. On the wet sheet chloramine T, 2 percent in water, was applied to the stains. All stains were reduced, and the pale ones were removed by this application.

The paper was dried under moderate pressure. It was then bathed again, and remaining stains were bleached with a 2½ percent solution of sodium hypochlorite on the wet paper. Thorough washing in a water bath was carried out after each application of bleaching solution. When dry, the paper was disinfected in an airtight chamber with thymol.

Appendix B · Special Means of Examination

A GREAT DEAL has been said about the scientific instruments and techniques which may aid in the examination of pictures; books have been published on some of them. Interest has been fomented by the prospect that they would help in efforts to authenticate works of art. The value of laboratory findings may, in some cases, have been exaggerated, but certain scientific procedures are regularly taken as means to find and record evidence on condition which is not visible by eye or with a simple magnifying lens. The following list describes the principal means that are available and indicates the range of their utility in the care of pictures.

Chemical Analysis. The study of samples of material by physical and chemical means is microscopic or microchemical. This is a necessity with the paint and ground, and these are the principal structural parts of pictures on which such analysis can give important information. In practice, the application of any reagents to the minute samples that can be afforded— usually these are barely visible to the eye—follows a general observation of the appearance of the sample and frequently an observation of its crystal character if it is a pigment or inert material.

Analytical means are qualitative. Spot reactions are the normal procedure, and a fund of experience is needed to recognize such reactions on the scale at which they occur. Medium, adhesive, and coating material are not as yet subject to any regular system of chemical test. Certain characteristic kinds of behavior can, however, be noticed. The natural resins are put into solution by most of the organic solvents, especially if aided by heat. For use on a microscope slide, solvents of lesser volatility are the more suitable; others disappear by evaporation before they have had time to take effect. Oils, unless combined with a high content of resin, are not affected by these solvents, but they are dissolved by dilute sodium hydroxide. Glues and gums are softened at least and may, with repeated application, dissolve in water, when heated in a water drop on a microscope slide. There have been numerous and sometimes successful explorations beyond these simple lines of behavior, and the microchemist is able to call upon a far more complicated series of tests.

Analytical method has gone much further with pigments and inert materials. Not to serve as a review of these reactions but merely to indicate what they are like, a description of a few of the most usual tests can be given. White lead, the basic lead carbonate, dissolves completely, rapidly, and with effervescence in dilute nitric acid. If the drop on the slide is warmed and dried rapidly, it leaves a characteristic formation of lead nitrate crystals. A copper green such as malachite, verdigris, or emerald green, will dissolve in dilute hydrochloric acid. The presence of copper can be confirmed from another part of the sample by the addition of water, followed by a small crystal of potassium ferrocyanide and, after that, by a small drop of hydrochloric acid. An easily recognized pinkish red envelope of copper ferrocyanide develops. Prussian blue turns brown on the addition of dilute sodium hydroxide. When next treated with dilute hydrochloric acid, it will usually regain its blue color. Identification of Prussian blue, like that of emerald green, zinc white, and an increasing number of modern pigments that are regularly used, is an important piece of evidence in discrimination between original and later paint. The relative date of the invention of Prussian blue can be fixed, and, since it is a complex material as well as a blue of desirable color strength, there is no reasonable chance that it was in use before the date of its known invention.

Color Analysis. Although precise means have been developed for the analysis of color from samples that can be placed in an instrument, direct comparison of the color located in the varied tones of a picture with samples having a definite specification, has not been extensively developed as yet. The only method of analysis which has been proposed for pictures is with an adaptation of the instrument known as the Lovibond Tintometer, a kind of colorimeter. The method was worked out with clear results by Rawlins at the National Gallery in London. From this instrument it was possible to derive numerical records of local tones in a picture and to follow any changes that occurred in those tones as a result of deterioration or of treatment. In general, color analysis consists of the measurement of a sample for the purpose of determining the relative amount of light in the different wave lengths of the visible spectrum which that sample is capable of reflecting. This can be given in figures of quantity for the different wave lengths or it can be recorded on a graph. Such a graph is drawn on coordinates in which the wave length is represented on the horizontal line and the amount of light reflected is shown on the vertical line. Spectroscopy runs into invisible radiations and is a means of recognizing chemical elements by their wave lengths in the electromagnetic spectrum.

Colorimetry. The colorimeter is an instrument which makes measurement of the color of light. Usually it requires observation to match an unknown sample against a tone which can be measured. It is probably most efficient for samples of materials that can be put into solution and studied by transmitted light. The beam that is to be measured and a beam of standard light are brought together in closely adjacent fields. In a trichromatic colorimeter the standard is supplied by three beams passed respectively through red, green, and blue filters and superimposed on a screen. The amount of each can be adjusted to a match. A monochromatic colorimeter has a prism through which white light is dispersed. Other colorimeters use liquids as standards. Measurement can be made of reflection, that is, light reflected from a surface rather than passed through a solution (see Color Analysis).

Color Measurement. All measurement of visual tone in pictures is based on means to record the quality and the quantity of light which can be reflected from a specific, uniform tonal area. The quantity is the total amount of light, regardless of color. Specific color is the quality of light reflected. A rough or approximate estimate of color measure for a given tone can be made by means of comparison with known samples. Such samples exist in the Munsell and the Ostwald color series and in numerous other systems which have been made for practical purposes. The measurement of color as a means to record one part of the condition of pictures has not been carried into routine practice (see Color Analysis). There is an opportunity for its further development and application to this field. Certain difficulties will have to be overcome if direct matching of samples with areas of pictures reaches a satisfactory procedure. One of these is the complication caused by different structures of paint, rich or glaze-like paint as against a mat surface. Another difficulty is the specular type of reflection from heavily coated paint and the influence of the tint of a coating on the color beneath it.

Grenz Ray Analysis. Many years after X rays were first used as a means of examining pictures, some experiments were made with the wave lengths that are slightly longer than X rays but still lie in the very high frequency region on the border between ultraviolet and X rays. The method is like radiography. Radiation goes through the picture, and relative densities are recorded on plates or films. These rays have been most effective with materials of slight density such as those in drawings and in illuminated manuscripts. In some instances later additions and changes have been made more conspicuous by this means, but little has been done to explore it and it is not yet used in routine procedure.

Infrared Photography. Plates or films for photography can be sensitized to record those radiations that are invisible to the human eye because they are longer than the waves in the long or red part of the spectrum. It has been found that these rays, when used in the photography of pictures, penetrate superficial layers of varnish and overpaint, under normal circumstances, at least farther than do the wave lengths to which the eye is sensitive. Special filters on the camera as well as special plates are used. The depth of penetration is only partial and is influenced by many factors. In addition, a very few pigments react in a specific way to infrared radiation. Minor losses from flaking and abrasion which may have been concealed by thin scumbles or glazes of rich paint are apt to be faintly exposed by an infrared photograph if it is carefully made. Overpaint itself is frequently shown in more marked degree.

Microchemical Analysis. Observations of the chemical reaction of materials in pictures have to be made microscopically (see Chemical Analysis), and a highly developed technique has been established for this. The samples taken are small, often hardly visible to the eye, and are placed on microscope slides where the reactions are produced by drops of the solutions needed. In some cases cross sections of minute chips of paint film are required as a means for defining the differences of layers and coatings; the chips, usually embedded in blocks of paraffin, are cut with a microtome to give a surface suitable for observations. The stage microscope is used for all of these observations, and normal magnifications are 50 to 200. Illumination is by either reflected or transmitted light as required. Physical observations on the shape and character of crystals and on solubility of adhesives and mediums are carried out at the same time.

Microscopy. In the examination of pictures microscopy is usually defined as the examination of minute samples of paint or other materials (see Microchemical Analysis and Chemical Analysis). As a routine matter, however, the surface of paint is examined with a microscope, usually a binocular, giving 5 to 50X. This is probably the most used and most useful instrument for examination. In a field magnified 10 to 25 times, the distinction between original and later paint can usually be observed, the existence of mold, grime, stains and other discolorations can be identified, and the earmarks of brittleness in a surface coating become apparent as fractures in that coating. Microscopy is occasionally used for special identification of materials such as wood, paper fibers, and other supports.

Microtome. A cutting instrument used to prepare cross sections of the paint layers for microscopic and microchemical examination.

Photomacrography. Fairly wide use has been made, for comparison purposes, of photographs of picture details enlarged from 2 to 10 times on the photographic film. The term "photomicrography" has often been kept for photographic records at much higher magnification, generally made of samples on a microscope slide. The distinction is one of degree and seems to exist largely for purposes of convenience. The observer gets no information from the photomacrograph beyond that available in the study of a picture surface with a binocular microscope. These photographs serve some purpose, however, in long-term comparison and in establishing a clear record.

Photomicrography. The photographic record of a microscope sample (see Microchemical Analysis and Photomacrography).

Quartz Lamp Examination. See Ultraviolet Examination.

Radiograph. The film or plate made by X rays passing through a picture and recording relative densities.

Radiography. A large number of terms has been used with changing favor and emphasis to cover the procedure of directing X rays through a picture on to a sensitized plate as a means of getting information about its structure and condition. Radiography, radiology, roentgenology, and X ray shadowgraphs are the most common among these terms. The radiation, of extremely high frequency, is produced by accelerating electrons in a vacuum by means of applied high voltage and having them strike a metal target from which the rays are emitted. The utility of X rays is limited both as to type of picture and as to the kind of evidence produced. The rays penetrate most of the components of a picture's construction and make a shadow darkening the plate as they strike through those materials. In a broad sense, the type of picture about which radiography gives satisfactory information is the picture produced in Europe and in the Western Hemisphere with white lead as a pigment. The other pigments, mixed with white or used without such a mixture, are so lacking in density that they have little impeding effect on these short radiations. Basic lead carbonate, however, is a very dense material and, since it is the common white in the pictures of the West from the Middle Ages until the nineteenth century, a sufficient density is usually present in these pictures to leave evident marks, shadows, where flaking, abrasion, or other loss may have occurred.

The greatest utility of radiography in the study of the condition of pictures is in the detection of such losses. There have been many cases, however, in which the presence of overpaint could be inferred from elements in a representation, seen in a radiograph but not apparent at the surface. It is also true that there may have been changes made by the painter of the picture and that concealment of parts was deliberate in the development of the work. Probably more has been expected of radiography than it could possibly supply in the way of evidence. It can not usually validate a signature or, in itself, furnish grounds for authentication. Previous repair of a painting is often made evident by radiography, particularly if there has been a transfer or extensive change in a support. Such repair is often an impediment to a clear radiographic record of the condition of paint and ground. Heavy fills of worm holes and the presence of a cradle or of a painted design on the reverse of a panel will confuse the contrasts of those densities which are the subject of concern. A means of overcoming a large part of this difficulty and an important step in the development of the radiography of pictures has been found by Rawlins of the National Gallery in

London, and by Pease of the Metropolitan Museum of Art in New York. This has the provisional name of traversed-focus radiography. It is contrived in such a way that exposure occurs while the picture is rotating and permits impediments back of the ground to be blurred and to lose their confusing emphasis. Radiography has been used effectively in Europe as a means of determining whether or not the larvae of beetles are active in a panel.

Radiology. See Radiography.

Raking-Light Examination. In normal diffuse light the conformation or the contours of the surface of a picture are often not clearly evident. These irregularities of surface which may reveal cleavage and other distortions can be brought into sharp relief by having a narrow beam of light thrown across the surface and in a plane parallel with it. In a dark room a single light source, narrowed to a slit and placed so that it rakes across a picture, will bring about this result. Such illumination is useful for photographic record.

Roentgenology. See Radiography.

Shadowgraph. See Radiograph.

Spectrograph. The instrument is used to record on a photographic film or plate the distribution of light caused by combustion of an unknown sample in an electric arc. The chemical elements have certain positions in the spectrum, determined by their discrete and characteristic wave lengths, and the use of spectrography is to establish those positions for a sample examined (see Spectroscopy).

Spectrometer. Rarely used in the examination of picture materials, the spectrometer is an instrument primarily for determining the index of refraction (see Spectroscopy).

Spectrophotometry. The spectrophotometric method of color analysis consists in illuminating a sample successively with beams of spectrum light, each of a single color, and measuring the proportion of such light as is reflected by the sample. The spectrophotometer is the instrument designed for this purpose (see Color Analysis). In the mechanics of one type of instrument, the reflectance of the sample is plotted mechanically as a curve. This instrument has not yet been used to record the color in pictures but has been made the means for an exact study of the colors of a wide range of pigments.

Spectroscopy. Spectroscopic analysis, the recognition of a chemical element by means of its characteristic group of wave lengths, is basic to spectrography and spectrometry. In the examination of picture materials—largely pigments and inert substances—emission spectra are used. The material to be analyzed is converted into an incandescent vapor by burning it in an electric arc. One instrument, the spectrograph, is devised to photograph the spectral distribution of the light that is produced. Spectroscopy is used mainly as a confirmation or as a substitute for microchemical identification.

Tintometer. A type of colorimeter which has been used in analyzing the reflectance of tones in pictures as a means of recording their condition— discoloration and response to removal of discolored materials (see Color Analysis).

Ultraviolet Examination. The production of radiation beyond the range visible to the human eye occurs in nature. The sun emits wave lengths shorter than those which can be seen. Various chemical elements, when acted on electrically, also emit short radiations. The most usual of these are carbon and mercury. Largely, the mercury arc has been the source of ultraviolet light for the examination of pictures. It is probably more efficient in a quartz tube than in glass, for the transmission of ultraviolet light by glass is very slight.

Any efficiency in this means of examination, however, depends not upon illumination alone but rather upon a phenomenon known as fluorescence. Many materials, when acted upon by short waves, are stirred into a secondary activity of their own and emit a weak light which goes by this name. This weak light is visible when the source is filtered. Some of the materials used in picturemaking show this behavior, and many of the materials and growths which cause damage to pictures have a certain fluorescence. A full analytical study of fluorescence in relation to pictures has not been made, and many of the observations under filtered ultraviolet light are indications rather than proofs. The following reactions can usually be noticed:

1. Surface coatings have a yellowish fluorescence which seems to increase with age.

2. Overpaint is apt to fluoresce less than the adjacent original paint, largely, it seems, because the overpaint lies above the first level of the surface coating.

3. There is little analytical distinction among the kinds of surface coating, but orange shellac or natural, unbleached shellac, rarely used on pictures, has a bright orange-colored fluorescence.

4. A very few pigments have a peculiar and strong fluorescence if they are exposed without a covering layer of surface coating; zinc white, for example, fluoresces a bright lemon yellow, and madder a salmon pink.

5. On paper supports the stains which may have been caused by an oily material will usually show a brighter fluorescence under ultraviolet light than will water stains.

6. Mold and foxed spots are given stronger contrast through fluorescence than through normal means of observation.

X Ray Shadowgraph. See Radiography.

Bibliography

Abbreviations:

TSFFA—Technical Studies in the Field of the Fine Arts

S in C—Studies in Conservation

Anonymous. *Report on the Deteriorating Effects of Modern Light Sources*, Metropolitan Museum of Art, New York, 1953.

Asperen de Boer, J. R. J. van. "Reflectography of Paintings Using an Infra-red Vidicon Television System," *S in C*, XIV (1969), 96–118.

Barnes, Norman F. "A Spectrophometric Study of Artists' Pigments," *TSFFA*, VII (1939), 120–38.

Beck, Walter. "Something about Pastel Technic and Its Permanence," *TSFFA*, II (1934), 119–23.

Blom, A. V. "Die Rissbildung in Anstrichen," *Farben-Zeitung*, XLII (1937), 409–10.

Boissonnas, Alain. "Relining with Glass-fiber Fabric," *S in C*, VI (1961), 26–30.

——— "The Treatment of Fire-blistered Oil Paintings," *S in C*, VIII (1963), 55–66.

Boissonnas, Pierre B. "Emploi du Vacuum pour les Tableaux sur Bois," *S in C*, IX (1964), 43–49.

Bradley, Morton C., Jr. *The Treatment of Pictures*, Cambridge, Massachusetts, 1951.

Bridgman, Charles F., Sheldon Keck, and Harold F. Sherwood. "The Radiography of Panel Paintings by Electron Emission," *S in C*, III (1958), 175–82.

Brommelle, N. S. "The Russell and Abney Report on the Action of Light on Water Colours," *S in C*, IX (1964), 140–52.

——— "Colour and Conservation," *S in C*, II (1955), 76–86.

Buck, Richard D. "A Note on the Effect of Age on the Hygroscopic Behavior of Wood," *S in C*, I (1952), 39–44.

——— "The Use of Moisture Barriers on Panel Paintings," *S in C*, VI (1961), 9–20.

Buck, Richard D., and George L. Stout. "Original and Later Paint in Pictures," *TSFFA* VIII (1940), 123–50.

Busch, Harold. "Vom richtigen und falschen Restaurieren," *Die Kunst*, XXXV (1934), 185–88.

Catalogue and Communications, *Exposition of Painting Conservation*, Brooklyn Museum, New York, 1962.

Cooper, B. S. "Fluorescent Lighting in Museums," *Museums Journal*, LIII (1954), 279–90.

Coremans, P. "Air Conditioning in Museums," *Museums Journal*, XXXVI (1936), 341–45.

Cornelius, F. du Pont. "Movement of Wood and Canvas for Paintings in Response to High and Low RH Cycles," *S in C*, XII (1967), 76–80.

Crawford, B. H., and D. A. Palmer. "Further Investigations of Colour Rendering and the Classification of Light Sources," *S in C*, VI (1961), 71–82.

Cursiter, Stanley. "Control of Air in Cases and Frames," *TSFFA*, V (1936) 109–16.

Cursiter, Stanley, and A. Martin de Wild. Four articles on picture relining: *TSFFA*, V (1937), 151–78; VI (1938), 174–79; VII (1938), 80–87; VII (1939), 191–95.

Eibner, Alexander. "Neue Wege zum Oberflächenschutz," *Farben-Zeitung*, XXXVI (1931), 1849–50, 1892–94; XXXVII (1931), 13–15, 88–90.

Feller, Robert L. "Dammar and Mastic Varnishes—Hardness, Brittleness, and Change in Weight upon Drying," *S in C*, III (1958), 162–74.

Feller, Robert L., Elizabeth H. Jones, and Nathan Stolow, *On Picture Varnishes and Their Solvents*, Reports Presented to the Seminar on Resinous Surface Coatings Sponsored by the Intermuseum Conservation Association, April 2–5, 1957, Oberlin, Ohio, 1959.

Gettens, Rutherford J., and Elizabeth Bigelow. "The Moisture Permeability of Protective Coatings," *TSFFA*, II (1932), 15–25.

Gettens, Rutherford J., Murray Pease, and George L. Stout. "The Problem of Mold Growth in Paintings," *TSFFA*, IX (1941), 127–43.

Gettens, Rutherford J. and George L. Stout. *Painting Materials, a Short Encyclopedia*, New York, 1942. (Dover reprint.)

Gregg, S. J. *The Surface Chemistry of Solids*, London, 1951.

Hanson, Fred S. "Resistance of Paper to Natural Aging," *The Paper Industry and Paper World*, XX (Feb. 1939).

Hatch, Aram H. "Notes on the Experimental Studies made for the Prevention of Mold Growth on Mural Paintings," *TSFFA*, II (1934), 129–37.

Heiber, W. "The Use of an Infra-red Image-converter for the Examination of Panel Paintings," *S in C*, XIII (1968), 145–49.

Hess, M. *Paint Film Defects—Their Causes and Cure*, London, 1951.

Hieronymi, Angelina. "Über Trübungen und Verdunkelungen von Gemälden," *Technische Mitteilungen für Malerei*, XLIX (1933), 35–37.

Ingen, W. B. van. "Notes on the Fungicidal Treatment of Paintings in the Canal Zone," *TSFFA*, I (1933), 143–54.

Keck, Caroline C. *A Handbook on the Care of Paintings for Historical Agencies and Small Museums*, Nashville, Tennessee, 1965.

Keck, Sheldon. "A Method of Cleaning Prints," *TSFFA*, V (1936), 117–26.

——— "Mechanical Alteration of the Paint Film," *S in C*, XIV (1969), 9–30.

Laurie, A. P. "Dévernissage des Tableaux Anciens et la Suppression des Repeints," *Mouseion*, XXV–XXVI (1934) 216–19.

——— "The Warping of Panels," *Museums Journal*, XXXII (1933), 389–91.

Margaritoff, Tasso. "A New Method for Removing Successive Layers of Painting," *S in C*, XII (1967), 140–46.

Masschelein-Kleiner, L., J. Heylen, and F. Tricot-Marckx, "Contribution à l'Analyse des Liants, Adhésifs et Vernis Anciens," *S in C*, XIII (1968), 105–21.

Mills, John S. "The Gas Chromatograph in Examination of Paint Media. Part I. Fatty Acid Composition and Identification of Dried Oil Films, *S in C*, XI (1966), 92–107.

Payne, H. F., and W. H. Gardner. "Permeability of Varnish Films," *Industrial and Engineering Chemistry*, XXIX (1937), 893–98.

Pease, Murray. "A Note on the Radiography of Paintings," *Bulletin of the Metropolitan Museum of Art*, IV (1946), 136–39.

Plenderleith, H. J. *The Conservation of Prints, Drawings, and Manuscripts*, London, 1937.

——— *The Conservation of Antiquities and Works of Art: Treatment, Repair, and Restoration*, London, 1956.

——— "The Examination and Preservation of Paintings: a Digest," *Museums Journal*, XXXII (1932), 308–10, 349–51; (1933), 388–89.

Plenderleith, H. J., and Stanley Cursitor. "The Problem of Lining Adhesives for Paintings—Wax Adhesives," *TSFFA*, III (1934), 90–113.

Plenderleith, H. J., and P. Philippot. "Climatology and Conservation in Museums" (compiled and edited; English and French), Centre International d'Études pour la Conservation et la Restoration des Biens Culturels, *Museum*, XIII (1960), No. 4, 202 ff.

Rawlins, F. Ian G. "The Control of Temperature and Humidity in Relation to Works of Art," *Museums Journal*, XLI (1942), 279–83.

——— "The Optical Properties of Some Common Varnishes," *TSFFA*, IV (1938), 180–82.

——— "Studies in the Colorimetry of Paintings," *TSFFA*, IV (1936), 179–86; V (1937), 150–56; IX (1941), 207–20; X (1942), 230–31.

Rorimer, James J. *Ultra-violet Rays and their Use in the Examination of Works of Art*, New York, Metropolitan Museum of Art, 1931.

Rosen, David. "A Wax Formula," *TSFFA*, III (1934), 114–15.

Rosegrant, Robert G. "Packing Problems and Procedures," *TSFFA*, X (1942), 138–56.

Ruhemann, Helmut. "A Record of Restoration," *TSFFA*, III (1934), 3–15.

——— "The Impregnation and Lining of Paintings on a Hot Table," *S in C*, I (1953), 73–76.

——— "Restoration of 'La Haie: Landscape near Arles' by Van Gogh," *S in C*, I (1953), 77 ff.

——— "Criteria for Distinguishing Additions from Original Paint," *S in C*, III (1958), 145–61.

——— "Experiences with Artificial Lighting of Paintings," *S in C*, VI (1961), 83–85.

——— *The Cleaning of Paintings, Problems and Potentialities*, London (Faber and Faber), 1968.

Sayre, Edward V., and Heather Lechtman. "Neutron Activation Autoradiography of Oil Paintings," *S in C*, XIII (1968), 161–85.

Slabczynski, Stefan. "The large Vacuum Hot Table for Wax Relining of Paintings in the Conservation Department of the Tate Gallery," *S in C*, V (1960), 1–16.

Stolow, Nathan. "The Measurement of Film Thickness and of Solvent Action on Supported Films," *S in C*, III (1957), 40–44.

Stout, George L., and Richard D. Buck. "Original and Later Paint in Pictures," *TSFFA*, VIII (1940), 123–50.

Stout, George L., and Rutherford J. Gettens, "The Problem of Lining Adhesives for Paintings," *TSFFA*, II (1933), 81–104.

Stout, George L., and Minna H. Horwitz. "Experiments with Adhesives for Paper," *TSFFA*, III (1934), 38–46.

Strain, D. E. R., Grace Kennely, and H. R. Dittmar. "Methacrylate Resins," *Industrial and Engineering Chemistry*, XXXI (1939), 382–87.

Straub, R. E., and S. Rees-Jones. "Marouflage, Relining, and the Treatment of Cupping with Atmospheric Pressure," *S in C*, II (1955), 55–63.

Sugden, Robert P. *Care and Handling of Art Objects*, New York, Metropolitan Museum of Art, 1946.

Thomson, Garry. "A New Look at Colour Rendering, Level of Illumination, and Protection from Ultraviolet Radiation in Museum Lighting," *S in C*, VI (1961), 49–70.

———— "Relative Humidity—Variation with Temperature in a Case Containing Wood," *S in C*, IX (1964), 153–69.

———— "Air Pollution—a Review for Conservation Chemists," *S in C*, X (1965), 147–67.

Tintori, Leonetto, Edward V. Sayre, and Lawrence J. Majewski. "Studies for the Preservation of the Frescoes by Giotto in the Scrovegni Chapel at Padua," *S in C*, VIII (1963), 37–54.

Wales, Carroll. "The Treatment of Wall Paintings at the Kariye Çamii," *S in C*, III (1958), 120–24.

Wehlte, K. *Werkstoffe und Techniken der Malerei*, Otto Maier Verlag, Ravensburg, 1967.

Weidner, Marilyn Kemp. "Damage and Deterioration of Art on Paper due to Ignorance and the Use of Faulty Materials," *S in C*, XII (1967), 5–25.

Wild, A. Martin de. *The Scientific Examination of Pictures*, London, 1929.

PLATE I

Fractures in a heavy coating of brittle varnish show as white lines and spots. This is a magnified photographic detail from an area of dark paint in an American portrait of about 1800.

PLATE II

Results of clearing away dark varnish and thin scumbled overpaint are evident in a photographic detail of a panel painting, Flemish, fifteenth century. These extraneous coatings have been cleared from the light strip that runs vertically through the left center. (Courtesy of the Museum of Fine Arts, Boston, and of *Technical Studies in the Field of the Fine Arts*.)

PLATE III

The discoloration caused by darkened surface coatings is evident in the strip at the extreme left of this magnified detail from an Italian painting of the eighteenth century.

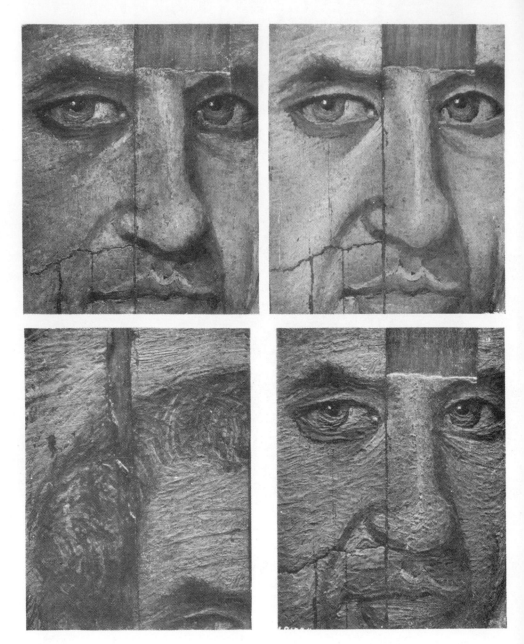

PLATE IV

Clearing of embedded grime from a Fayum portrait, *c.* 100 A.D., is shown partly completed in the upper left detail; completed, in the upper right. Below are raking-light photographs after treatment. The surface character of the wax paint has not been injured by mechanical removal of the grime. (Courtesy of *Technical Studies in the Field of the Fine Arts.*)

PLATE V

Dark splotches, noticeable in forehead and neck particularly, are from overpaint. The detail is from an "Entombment of Christ," a panel painting of the fifteenth century. The overpaint, in a resinous medium, probably matched the original paint when it was put on, but turned brown with time. (Courtesy of *Technical Studies in the Field of the Fine Arts.*)

PLATE VI

Magnified photographic detail from a Flemish painting, fifteenth century, shows loss of paint from wear or from rubbing in a few places along the cracks and a heavy deposit of grime in the hollows of the paint. The detail is ten times actual size.

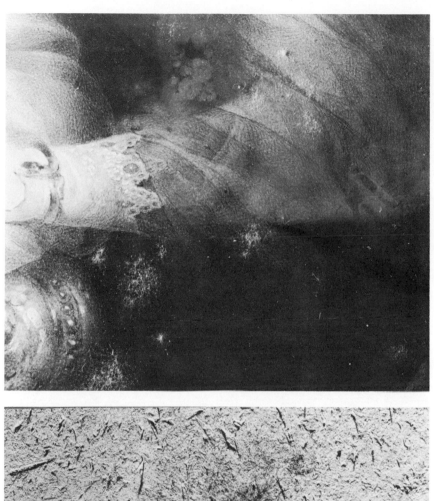

PLATE VII

Clumps of mold showing white against the darker paint are seen in the upper photograph, a detail from a miniature of the nineteenth century. Much magnified, a similar clump is photographed in the lower detail as it was found on a work in pastel.

PLATE VIII

Mold growing in an oil painting attached to a wall is shown in the upper detail from the frieze in the Administration Building, Panama Canal. The lower photograph is the same detail after removal of the mold. (Courtesy of *Technical Studies in the Field of the Fine Arts.*)

PLATE IX

Loss of paint from plaster, characteristic of the way this defect occurs, is represented by a photographic detail from a Persian wall painting. The irregular white blemishes are the result of minute flaking combined with rubbing or abrasion.

PLATE X

Discoloration of ground is combined with loss by chalking or abrasion in a granular blue paint. The detail is from a panel painting, Italian, fourteenth century. The light areas are chalked to the ground. The dark stains (at the tips of the arrows) are between the ground and the blue paint layer. (Courtesy of *Technical Studies in the Field of the Fine Arts.*)

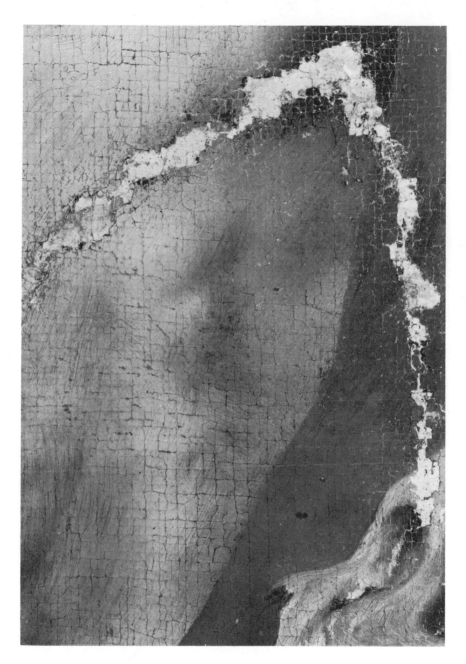

PLATE XI

A seventeenth-century Spanish painting shows the usual jagged mark of an old tear. Such tears invariably cause loss of paint and ground which flake along the edges. In this instance the losses are filled with new ground.

PLATE XII

Treatment of a broken and pitted fragment of Chinese wall painting has recovered some of the design. Holes and cracks seen in the upper photograph are filled, in the lower, with clay toned to raise the value and reduce the contrast. This allows the drawing to be seen without confusion. (Courtesy of *Technical Studies in the Field of the Fine Arts*.)

PLATE XIII

Overpainting and compensation of paint losses are compared in a Florentine altarpiece, c. 1300 (detail). At the top, losses have been roughly painted over. The middle photograph shows the extent of actual loss. In the lower, losses have been compensated without overpainting and with no added drawing. (Courtesy of The Isabella Stewart Gardner Museum, Boston.)

PLATE XIV

Two types of cleavage are indicated in this detail from a Florentine panel painting of the fourteenth century. In the upper part the large buckled areas, like a gabled roof, are loosened between ground and support and pushed up by shrinkage of the wood panel. The lower and left-hand parts have buckling characteristic of cleavage in the upper layer of the ground or between the ground and the paint.

PLATE XV

Buckling in the ground layer is brought out sharply by raking illumination. This is a detail from a German painting on canvas, *c.* 1800. (Courtesy of *Technical Studies in the Field of the Fine Arts.*)

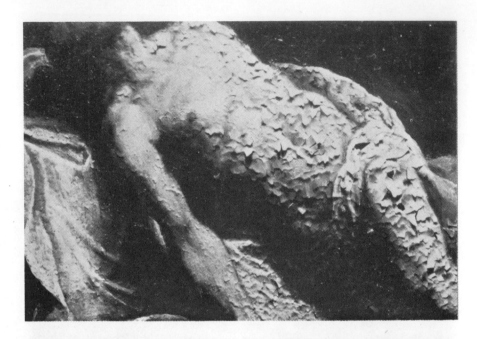

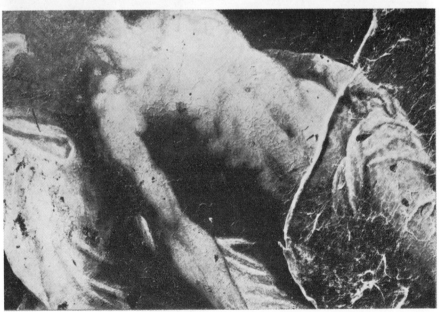

PLATE XVI

Extreme loosening or cleavage of paint from a stone support is represented by the upper detail from an Italian painting of the seventeenth century. The cause was the poor bond between paint and stone and the shrinkage of heavy varnish. The lower detail is from a photograph made during reattachment. (Courtesy of *Technical Studies in the Field of the Fine Arts*.)

PLATE XVII

The relation between the amount of damage to wood by worms (beetle larvae)
and worm holes through the paint is illustrated in a detail from an Italian panel
painting of the fifteenth century. In the upper part a few worm holes are seen
perforating the paint layer. The lower part is a small area of the wood underneath,
photographed from the reverse after a portion of it had been removed during the
process of reconstruction.

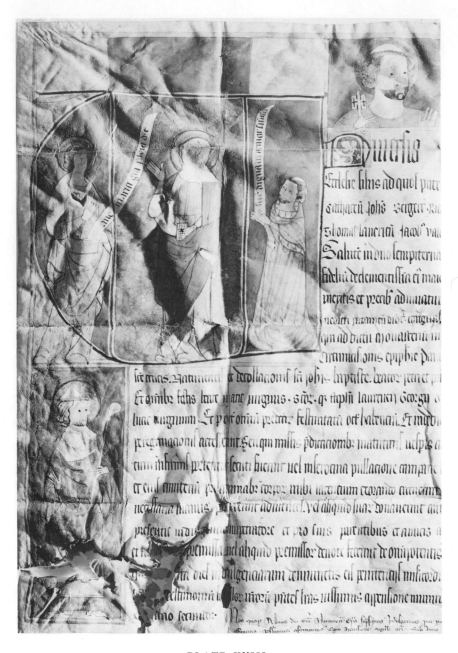

PLATE XVIII

Distortion of a vellum or parchment support is caused partly by folding, as noticeable in the rectangular creases, and partly by mounting, which has brought about the wrinkles at the edges. This is a detail from a French illuminated manuscript of the fourteenth century.

PLATE XIX

Discoloration with the pattern of wood grain is brought out in the upper photograph, a detail made by ultraviolet light. The work is a Spanish print of *c.* 1800. The lower photograph, made under normal light, is of the reverse. The stain was caused by contact with a wood backing.

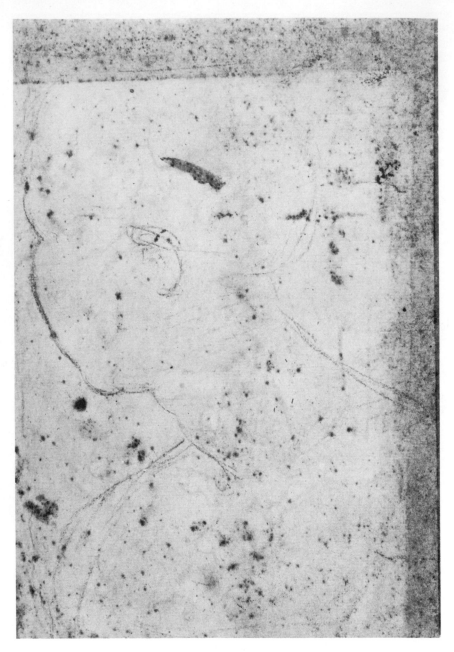

PLATE XX

Stain of a paper support from contact with the mount shows as an irregular, dark strip in the upper and right-hand edges of a detail from a drawing, Italian, early sixteenth century. Dark spots are largely from former mold growth, a discoloration known as foxing.

PLATE XXI

Water stain in the paper support, in the ground, and in the chalky paint is evident in a detail from a group portrait in pastel, American, early nineteenth century.

PLATE XXII

Reverse of the canvas support of a picture is photographed during preparation for relining, as described by Cursiter and De Wild. Above is the former relining fabric, partly torn off. Next it is a layer of the glue adhesive which attached it. The dark rectangle in the lower right is the original support with the glue layer removed. (Courtesy of *Technical Studies in the Field of the Fine Arts.*)

PLATE XXIII

One method of panel reconstruction is with linen and redwood strips held together by a wax adhesive which contains filling and inert materials. The photograph shows application of such a panel to a large painting in the process of transfer.

PLATE XXIV

A special case-frame for a large panel painting is afforded under British Patent Specification No. 396439, designed by Messrs. Wilsdon and Burridge and described by Mr. Stanley Cursiter, director of the National Gallery of Scotland, Edinburgh. Trays of salts in the base keep an equilibrium of relative humidity with a moderate circulation of air. (Courtesy of *Technical Studies in the Field of the Fine Arts.*)

Index